Fujita Seiko

Fujita Seiko

The Last Koga Ninja

Phillip T. Hevener

Editor: Sarah Burke

PREFACE

Phillip Hevener has done a great deal of research into the Koga ryu ninjutsu. This came about because of the claims made by persons professing expertise in Koga ryu and an attempt to confirm or deny those claims. His research into the last possible Grand Master Seiko Fujita discovered some very enlightening facts. This last Master of a Koga ryu stated in his memoirs that he would not pass on his ninjutsu knowledge to anyone. Since this is the last possible source, it does call to question all those who claim to come from a Koga tradition. I think you will find Mr. Hevener's facts both interesting and enlightening, I know I did.

Edward H. Martin
15th Dan Bujinkan ninjutsu

PROLOGUE

In attempting to write a biography of Fujita Seiko, I uncovered several interesting and seemingly contradictory factors. The first is that while Fujita was known for his claim to be "the last ninja," little substantive biographical information exists in ninjutsu circles to construct a picture of his career. Indeed, in the modern context, with ninjutsu existing only in the guise of the Bujinkan, and Fujita's name often being used to substantiate dubious claims of so-called "Koga" practitioners, much of his reputation, as understood by his contemporaries, has been obscured. Thus, as a member of the Bujinkan, I have, as much as possible, allowed the original sources to speak for themselves. The major reason for this decision is that I harbor the suspicion that our understanding of ninjutsu and budo in general today is affected by the Western preconceptions of ninjutsu that have developed since Stephen K. Hayes returned from Japan in 1980.

This is compounded by the fact that much of the completely original information in this work relating to Fujita Seiko comes to us from those connected to the Iwata family (Shito-Kai), Fujita's spiritual inheritors. I was therefore bound to present a picture of Fujita that did not diverge from their understanding of him. That being said, I presented the picture suggested by the documentation provided and anecdotal information. Another fact that also confines any researcher delving into the career of Fujita Seiko is the fact that Fujita himself is the only source that speaks about his early career. This fact, along with the general unfamiliarity of the martial arts community with factual details of Fujita's career outside of the ninja boom, indicated that I should use primary sources, of which Fujita's own writings, *Koga Ryu Ninja Ichidaiki*, *Ninjutsu Hiroku*, and *Watashi Wa Ninjutsu Tsukai*, and his obituary, The Last Ninja Disappears, were the main ones.

Another interesting trend in the martial arts community related to Fujita Seiko is the willingness of so-called koryu practitioners to accept his claim to being "the last ninja" while virulently opposing the claims of the Bujinkan Soke, Dr. Hatsumi Masaaki. This situation aside, koryu sources added an interesting window into Fujita's career that helps to balance the way he is viewed, especially when we consider the dynamics of the Western ninja boom. Indeed, most of the arts for which Fujita held licensing were of this particular ilk.

The last source, mentioned earlier, that proved surprisingly to be the most informative was the Okinawan arts of Shito-ryu Karate-do and Yuishinkai Karate-jutsu. It turned out that these sources held the key to Fujita's much-discussed eclectic streak, his oft-conjectured inheritor, and the fate of his Wada-ha Koga-ryu ninjutsu. This discovery involved a significant conceptual readjustment on my part, departing from a Bujinkan perspective, and proved to be the solution to the puzzle laid out before me.

In the end the work I have compiled is a look into the career of Fujita Seiko that is slanted heavily toward one group of martial artists that knew him during his lifetime. This view is accompanied by Fujita's own vision of his career as depicted in the sources mentioned. I am convinced that I have presented a genuine picture of Fujita—one that he would have recognized and that his chosen inheritor, Iwata Manzo, would have endorsed. I have no doubt, however, that owing to the combination of the Japanese bent for secrecy and Fujita's eclectic nature, much about him remains to be discovered. What is beyond doubt, though, is that the fate of Fujita's ninjutsu and other arts is addressed in this work.

Finally, I would urge all researchers interested in the martial arts in general, and ninjutsu in particular, to use this work as a springboard to forming a complete picture of the man whose name is ever-present in ninjutsu circles, and who has for so long been what his student Iwata Manzo called "the mysterious man of the martial arts."

UNSETTLED YOUTH

Fujita Seiko, a famous, influential, and controversial Japanese figure of the early 20th century, is remembered as an author, researcher, martial arts authority, staunch nationalist, dabbler in eccentric religions, and, as Fujita himself would have liked to be remembered, the 'last ninja.' Fujita was born in the Asakusa area of a small town called Istuka-shi, now a district of Tokyo, on August 13, 1899. Fujita's given name at birth was Isamu, but he changed it to Seiko during adolescence, a practice common in Japanese culture.[1] The Fujitas were a family of accomplished martial artists who belonged to Japan's esteemed warrior class, and as such, they entered the 20th century with all the privileges available to what was then Japan's dominant class.

Fujita's father, Fujita Morinosuke, originally intended to become a researcher in the medical sciences and secured a position as a doctor's assistant at Sapporo Hospital, where he received gradual promotions leading up to the position of Director of Shibetoro Hospital. However, Morinosuke found that he enjoyed drinking and socializing and therefore did not enjoy working in an area that was then considered a backwater. So he resigned and returned to Edo, where he secured a job as a prison guard on Ishikawa Island. Morinosuke then went on to find his life's calling when he became a policeman.[2] He eventually became a famous policeman with the Tokyo Metropolitan Police Department, where he used his expertise in the art of Ichiden-ryu Hojojutsu, an art that emphasized capturing and binding opponents. Morinosuke, known for his skill in apprehending criminals, retired in 1912 with the rank of inspector and ended his career with a tally of more than 3000 arrests, including the capture of 8 criminals who eventually received the death penalty, and 25 criminals who received life terms. Fujita's obituary mentioned that Morinosuke's acclaim was such that a song was composed to celebrate his exploits: "Detective Fujita is scarier than ogres, demons and monsters."[3]

The patriarch of the Fujita clan was Fujita's paternal grandfather, Fujita Shintazaemon (nicknamed Shinosuke),[4] who was the 13th head of the Fujita clan's ancestral martial art: Wada-ha Koga-ryu Ninjutsu. The Fujita family, who by some estimates practiced this art for 500 years, had, with the advent of peace, entered the employment of the Tokugawa Shogunate as spies.[5] The Fujita family included Rokugo,

Fujita's older brother, who was 5 years his senior, and an older sister who died when Fujita was 4 years old and whose name goes unstated in Fujita's autobiography.[6]

Several persons and events in Fujita's early life were to have lasting effects on his development. Foremost among them was Shintazaemon, his grandfather, from whom Fujita learned the foundation of his martial arts skills. Shintazaemon realized early that Fujita possessed the intelligence and athleticism to be a ninja. He noticed that his grandson was active and energetic from the time he was a baby, twice witnessing the baby Fujita fall down some stairs without injuring himself. Shintazaemon taught Fujita, at age 3, walking and jumping techniques associated with ninjutsu and other Japanese budo traditions, including lessons on how to commit hara-kiri (seppuku).[7] Morinosuke never interfered with Shintazaemon's budo training of Fujita, and Shintazaemon would become the most influential figure and role model in his grandson's life.

The second defining event in Fujita's early life occurred at about the age of 5, when he had a near-death experience caused by a bout of diphtheria. The disease caused Fujita's throat to swell, cutting off air to his lungs, resulting in cardiac arrest, and a doctor declared Fujita dead.[8] His mother, Tori, unwilling to accept the doctor's declaration, took her son into her arms and thrust a pipe down his throat to assist him in breathing. Miraculously, after a few minutes, Fujita came back to life and was subsequently viewed by his family as the beneficiary of divine intervention. This experience led the Fujita family to spoil and coddle Fujita, which led the young boy to become unruly and violent. His family attempted to tame Fujita's volatile temper by making him take magotaro mushi, a concoction of dried insects prescribed to treat fiery temperaments, according to Chinese medicine. Fujita despised the prescription, and only his grandfather could compel him to take it, because of the master-teacher relationship that existed between them. Although Fujita credited this experience with aiding his later martial arts success, it did little to calm his temper.[9]

Fujita's volatile temper is documented in a story that Fujita himself relayed in his 1968 memoir, *Koga Ryu Ninja Ichi Dai Ki*. He recalled that one winter's day his older brother, Rokugo, was surrounded and beaten by a group of about eight 15-year-old boys. Rokugo was finally able to escape, but only after his earlobes had been partially torn off, his neck and face bloodied, and his clothes in tatters. Fujita was so enraged by the attack on his brother that he grabbed his father's sword and raced to the area where Rokugo had been attacked. Fujita recounted, "I rapidly located my brother's assailants, around eight of them, boys of about 15 and 16, who were amusing themselves by striking each other with wooden swords."[10] When Rokugo's attackers saw Fujita approaching with a real blade, they fled. According to Fujita, he had no problem catching them. The fearful cries of his brother's assailants led eleven neighborhood farmers to run to their assistance, but Fujita saw those intervening as additional attackers. Eleven people were injured before he was subdued.

As a result of this incident, Fujita's parents sent him to a Buddhist temple at Daiji-dera, in Itsuka-shi, in the hopes that the monks' pacifist ways would soothe the young

maverick's temperament. Not long after the incident, Fujita's father was transferred from the police department in Oume to Itsuka-shi, a move that Fujita believed was a direct result of his actions against his brother's assailants.[11]

Fujita's time at the temple would also serve to influence his later life. From the point of view of a little child, Fujita remembered the temple as large and old. He remembered the temple and its ten monks, but most of all, he was most struck by the Buddhist statue of Emma, the "King of Hell,"[12] that stood in front of the main temple complex. Equally memorable was the statue of Shokka-baa, an emaciated and frightening old lady, whose task it was to cut away the clothes of the deceased as they journeyed down the river of death.

During his time at the temple, Fujita remembered being given a Buddhist name, although he was unable to recall it. He did remember that he was also referred to as "Shinpochi," or "lowest student."[13] His daily routine at the temple consisted of holding the bowls of all the monks and students as they were served miso, followed by the sweeping of the temple yard, which was difficult for a six-year old-boy. After his physical chores were completed, Fujita was required to recite a Buddhist sutra called "kaigebun." Only after completing these three tasks was he finally allowed to eat breakfast. If the daily temple schedule included a funeral ceremony, Fujita was required to assist in the preparations, by offering tea to the guests, arranging their shoes at the entrance, and assisting the abbot in whatever other responsibilities he saw fit to delegate to "Shinpochi."

After his first ten days at the temple, Fujita wanted to go home, because he found it difficult to endure the strict temple regimen. However, Fujita knew that leaving the temple would raise his father's ire, since he had been placed there in the hopes of rehabilitating his delinquent spirit. Gradually, he adjusted to the temple's daily routine and even started to become his normal self again, as the following story illustrates.

One day, as a result of Fujita's mischievous behavior, the abbot punished him by locking him in the room where the statue of Emma stood. Fujita was terrified by the large statue and cried incessantly for an hour. Upon reflection, he realized that the statue never moved, and he gradually lost his fear of Emma, which he soon demonstrated. When the other students finally came to check on him, they found Fujita standing on top of the statue, urinating from his perch. Fujita records that when he attempted to descend, he accidentally broke a piece of the statue, which only served to increase his defiance.

After the incident, Fujita seemed to fear nothing, and his delinquent behavior increased dramatically. From that point forward, any hope that the temple regimen would improve Fujita's disposition appeared to be a vain hope, and his misdeeds increased to such an extent that the abbot finally ordered him to return home. He was almost seven years old when he returned to his family and as far from being rehabilitated as when he was first sent away. Unbeknownst to him, a personal tragedy would soon intervene that would tame his fiery temperament for good and set him on the path he would follow for the rest of his life.

LIVING WITH THE YAMABUSHI

On Fujita's seventh birthday, August 13, 1906, Fujita's mother, Tori, the person from whom he believed he inherited his personality, died suddenly of a hemorrhage of the large intestine and colon. The young Fujita was grief-stricken and wondered if there was some unseen meaning in the fact that his mother had died on his birthday. In his memoirs Fujita recalled that after his mother died, he wandered aimlessly in the hills around his family home. It was here that Fujita came in contact with the Yamabushi, strange mountain ascetics who made pilgrimages to secluded mountains that they believed were the source of mysterious powers that animated nature.

One day, Fujita encountered a group of three Yamabushi on their way up the mountains, and he decided to follow them without informing his family. When the three Yamabushi entered the cedar forest, they looked back and noticed that Fujita was following them. They asked him who he was and told him to go home. Fujita ignored their insistent demands that he return to his family and kept following them.

In spite of the extreme hardship of the journey, Fujita continued to follow the ascetics, even though his knees were buckling with each step, and his body was drenched in sweat. Despite his extreme exhaustion, Fujita knew he had to persist in following the Yamabushi, since he realized he was too far away from home to find his way back. While Fujita was focused on keeping pace with his three strange companions, he noticed that they were able to walk quickly even where there was no road because they followed special markers left by other Yamabushi on previous trips up the mountain. These markers and signs were varied and ranged from knots tied in the grass, to branches woven together in a special fashion, to etchings left on trees that indicated the direction of travel. At times, these markers also relayed the number of travelers who had come that way, as well as how long the travelers had stayed.

As Fujita followed his strange new companions, he lost track of time and could not tell whether the journey had lasted one or two days. They finally arrived at a house where an elderly Yamabushi lived. Fujita thought that this old man with a beard that stretched down to his solar plexus looked like a Sennin, the Japanese equivalent of an immortal.

The place to which Fujita had followed the Yamabushi was Mount Mitsumine, in the Kanto district. It was a place the Yamabushi considered sacred, and many of their

sect ventured to this place to perform esoteric rituals lasting months at a time. Fujita slept under trees in the open air and awoke each morning to the empowering rays of the mountain sunlight. According to the Yamabushi tradition, the elements of nature were considered to possess magical properties and fire was considered to be the most sacred element in nature. As a result, the Yamabushi were forbidden to use fire without special permission from their abbot.

Fujita recounts that on warm days the abbot harnessed the power of fire by using a primitive magnifying glass. On rainy or cloudy days, the abbot created fire by rubbing a piece of bamboo against a tree. Fujita also noticed that instead of a rice cooker, the Yamabushi cooked rice with a furoshiki, a large square cloth that they also used to carry various things. The Yamabushi would put the rice in the furoshiki and bury it underground. They would then build a fire above the buried cloth, and the rice would cook while the Yamabushi chanted and chatted. The eating of rice, Fujita recollected, was a sign of a novice among the Yamabushi. Those who had practiced for several years ate very little rice, subsisting mostly on tree bark and wild nuts. The truly accomplished Yamabushi—those who had practiced for decades—were reputed to have become Sennin and were said to be able to suck dew and haze from the air for sustenance.

Fujita recalled that all his Yamabushi companions wore geta-wooden clogs similar to those common among the Japanese of his day. However, unlike ordinary geta, which are supported by two thick wooden soles, those worn by the Yamabushi were supported by only one sole, which was slanted in such a manner as to make it easier to climb mountains. In addition, Fujita noticed that the Yamabushi also carried triton shells, which were used as a sort of horn to signal when it was time to recite sutra. The Yamabushi carried the triton shells most of the time, and they used them at least three times a day—morning, noon, and night—to gather the ascetics for their arcane rituals. Fujita even witnessed a Yamabushi climbing a tree with one hand while holding the triton shell in the other.

Other rituals that Fujita witnessed during his stay with the Yamabushi included walking barefoot through fire, immersing hands in boiling water, and practicing jojutsu, a short-staff martial art favored by the Yamabushi. It was here that Fujita first practiced jojutsu, and he remembered that it proved to be very useful in a street fight years later. The *Bugei Ryuha Daijiten,* Japan's official martial arts encyclopedia, records that Fujita learned jojutsu from a Shugenja (Yamabushi) named Daien (Great Circle), and this art, Daien-ryu, teaches Bo and Ken (staff and sword).[14] Other Yamabushi practices that Fujita heard of were claims that they were able to walk up to 150 miles a day, traveling lightly, and up to 50 miles a day, carrying a heavy load.

Fujita noted that he later learned that walking quickly for long distances was also a skill used by the ninja. What perhaps surprised Fujita most was that on Mount Mitsumine, the Yamabushi appeared to be able to contact other Yamabushi located in places as far away as Mount Hakuzan and Mount Shiroyama, in the Kaga district, or Mount Ukokuzan in the Ugo district, by exchanging what he believed were non-verbal signals. Fujita believed that the Yamabushi could tell how many Yamabushi were coming to Mount Mitsumine, and from where they departed, before they arrived. Fujita's experiences with the Yamabushi convinced him that all human beings had paranormal capacities and that the Yamabushi had discovered how to channel these abilities through their esoteric rituals.

Fujita believed that he was perhaps the youngest person to have ever had the opportunity to practice with the Yamabushi. He recounts that he was well cared for and that the Yamabushi were fascinated with his ability to endure their regimen. Moreover, he recalled how surprised the Yamabushi were at how rapidly he memorized sutra, became adept at their jojutsu techniques, and adapted to immersing his hands in boiling water. These strange abilities and rituals would remain a part of Fujita's repertoire, and later in life, he would often demonstrate amazing feats of endurance and tolerance of pain that many attributed to his interaction with the Yamabushi.

After Fujita had been with the Yamabushi for about 100 days, the leaves on Mount Mitsumine began to change color, from green to brown, and the mornings and afternoons had become much colder. One day, while he was sitting and watching the Yamabushi reciting sutra and walking through fire, he heard someone call "hey, Isamu," and he turned around to see his father and his brother approaching. Since his disappearance, Morinosuke and Rokugo had searched for him incessantly, even soliciting police assistance in searching for him. The police concluded that Fujita was probably dead, after failing to find him in towns, forests, rivers, and nearby mountains.

After two months of searching, Morinosuke's neighbors told him that his son was dead and that he should stop looking for him. They believed that because they could not find his body, Fujita must have been spirited away by kami kakushi (hidden spirits). Morinosuke did not believe this and continued to search for his son, who he had a strange feeling was still alive. Using the expertise that came with being a policeman, Morinosuke searched the mountains around Chichibu and finally found his son.

It was the end of November, almost four months after Fujita had first left home, and he did not want to leave the Yamabushi. Nonetheless, Fujita was forced to return home to his family and was scolded all the way back by Morinosuke and Rokugo. Morinosuke was extremely angry that Fujita had worried and inconvenienced his police colleagues, friends, and neighbors. Fujita's grandfather, however, attempted to calm Morinosuke and shielded Fujita from his father's anger. Shintazaemon was very interested in Fujita's experiences with the Yamabushi and was attentive every time Fujita recalled his experiences. Fujita remembered Shintazaemon saying, "You had many good practices. Good. Good."[15]

THE LAST DISCIPLE OF THE WADA-HA

A few days after his return home from his 100-day adventure with the Yamabushi, Fujita was approached by Shintazaemon, who said to him:

> "You have the talent to be a ninja. I would like to teach you ninjutsu.
>   What do you think?"
> "I will," replied the young Fujita, without much reflection upon the matter.
> The old man continued, "But the training is going to be very hard for you.
>   Can you do it?"
> Fujita replied, "I can handle it."
> Shintazaemon pressed on: "It is better to say no if you don't have enough
>   confidence to complete the training. Are you sure you can do it?"
> Fujita responded, "I am sure."
> "Then perform Kincho," Shintazaemon instructed his grandson.

Kincho is the samurai way of swearing an oath by ritually crossing the blades of two swords. For the ceremony, Shintazaemon wore a long sword and gave Fujita a smaller one. Together Shintazaemon and Fujita performed the ritual, solemnly vowing to uphold the principles of the Wada-ha. Fujita thus entered into a tradition that spanned 14 generations, stretching back over 500 years into Japan's feudal past.[16]

Fujita was no longer simply Shintazaemon's grandson, but instead the disciple of the 13th patriarch of Wada-ha Koga-ryu Ninjutsu. According to the *Bugei Ryuha Daijiten*, the Wada-ha branch of Koga ninjutsu was founded by Wada Iga-No-Kami Koremasa, a direct ancestor of Fujita's. The encyclopedia also records that the Wada-ha was part of the Minami-yama Rokke (six strong families), also known as Wada Iga-shu, a subgroup within the 53 families that made up the Koga ninjutsu tradition.[17] Additional substantiation of a ninjutsu family named Wada from the precise region and time that Fujita claims exists in the historical record. Indeed, the author Stephen Turnbull records the following: "The Wada family, for example, controlled a series of mountain-top fortresses along a river valley, and Wada (Iga-No-Kami) Koremasa (1536-83) was sufficiently strong enough in Koga to give refuge there to the future shogun Yoshiaki after the suicide of his brother Ashikaga Yoshiteru in 1565."[18]

Fujita himself claimed that Koga-ryu Ninjutsu originated with the Isomi clan, which was composed of 21 sub-clans. These were further divided into four main houses: the Shonai Sanke (3), the Kashiwagi Sanke (3), the Kitayama Kuie (9), and the Minami-yama Rokke (6), Fujita's own house, loyal to the Wada Iga Daimyo (lord). Fujita went on to say that his family arrived in Edo with the Wada Iga Daimyo, to work as onmmitsumawari-doshin, spies, for Wada Iga's master, Tokugawa Ieyasu.[19] The onmitsumawari-doshin were part of the doshin, low-ranking bushi (warriors) who were divided into sanmawari (three patrols), two of which were uniformed (jomawari and rinjimawari), and the onmitsumawari, who were responsible for surveillance and intelligence gathering. The onmitsumawari performed their seemingly innocuous tasks for the Tokugawa, often posing as tradesmen or common laborers. The position of onmitsumawari was hereditary, generally being passed from father to son, although an application still had to be placed with the Machi-bugyo (town magistrate).[20] The onmitusmawari were often deployed across Japan to spy on the local Daimyo, to ensure their loyalty to the shogunate. Fujita singled out Kanda in Tokyo as the area where Tokugawa's Koga operatives settled and pointed to its sub-section of Koga-shi as the focal point of their activities and influence.[21]

Fujita would later explain in his memoirs that even if one was born into a ninjutsu family, one was not necessarily destined to inherit the knowledge and skills of the ninja. This fact is illustrated by the example of Morinosuke, who, although he went on to an illustrious career as a policeman, was not chosen by Shintazaemon to carry on the family tradition. Being chosen to be trained in the art of ninjutsu depended on possessing three very basic qualities: being honest and having a sense of justice, being intelligent, and being able to move quickly.[22]

TRAINING WITH THE MASTER

Having performed Kincho, Fujita was called into his grandfather's room to begin training. He had often heard stories of the ninja from both his father and grandfather and was both excited and nervous about what Shintazaemon was going to teach him. "Sit down," Shintazaemon said, as Fujita entered the room. It seemed to Fujita that his grandfather was much more serious and stern than usual. Shintazaemon reached over to a nearby table and picked up a piece of cotton, which he licked and placed on Fujita's nose. Although Fujita was nervous, he started to laugh at what his grandfather had just done. "Why do you laugh?" demanded Shintazaemon. "Because of this," answered Fujita, pointing to his nose, and just as he did, the cotton fell off. "This is the first practice. Pick it up and put it back on your nose." The aim of this first technique, called "Seisoku," was to teach Fujita how to control his breathing so that the piece of cotton would stay on his nose throughout the entire exercise. In the field this would allow the ninja to hide extremely close to an opponent, without the sounds of his breathing giving his position away. The ability to maintain an even breathing pattern during times of both physical exertion and at rest was vital to the ninja of the Wada-ha.[23]

The second set of lessons Fujita learned from Shintazaemon involved toughening the legs and feet so that he would be able to travel long distances on the tips of his toes for maximum speed, as the Yamabushi did in their mountain rituals. After about a month of walking on his tiptoes, Fujita became accustomed to the practice. His grandfather then introduced new methods. The next foot exercise involved walking on the outside edge of the feet, with the soles facing each other. This exercise caused Fujita a great deal of pain around the ankle joints and the surrounding area. Two days later, while practicing this new and painful exercise, Fujita heard a dull pop and fell to the floor with a broken ankle.[24] Fujita recorded that one cannot usually walk with such an injury; however, Shintazaemon set the bone immediately and rubbed it with a cream that smelled like vinegar. Two hours later Fujita no longer felt the pain, and the swelling on his ankle started to dissipate.

However, Fujita was sure that he was through with training for the day, so he was surprised when Shintazaemon said, "You broke your ankle, but you can still use your hands."[25] By this time, Shintazaemon had started to teach him finger-toughening techniques that involved thrusting his hands into sand to develop the ability to penetrate flesh and muscle. Fujita recorded that this was a vital skill on which the ninja depended. When he first started this phase of his training, he found the pain difficult to endure, since his fingers would bleed from the friction of the sharp grains of sand against his skin. After Fujita had trained daily with sand for about a month, Shintazaemon replaced the sand with gravel, and the process of becoming accustomed to this new medium unfolded as it had with the sand, until the gravel was finally replaced with clay. Once Fujita had become used to the clay, Shintazaemon instructed him to continue this training by striking the hard, packed ground. Fujita mentioned that the ninja of the Wada-ha were reputed, by virtue of this practice, to be able to sever an opponent's throat or to pluck out his ribs using only the fingers.[26]

The strengthening of the fingers was therefore fundamental to Fujita's training. This practice not only manifested itself in the manner described above, but Fujita also described techniques whereby the ninja would hang from a lattice, gripping it with only two fingers, and thus be able to move suspended only by his fingers, across a room the length of eight tatami (bamboo) mats in two to three minutes.[27]

Fujita repeated this regimen every day, and after a couple of months, Shintazaemon added a jumping technique to Fujita's afternoon training. Shintazaemon explained that there were six directions of jumping: forward, backward, high, broad, slanting, and sideways. Shintazaemon demonstrated an example of one of these types of jumping techniques by climbing a tree and leaping from a height that was about three times as high as an ordinary house. Although Shintazaemon's demonstration surprised Fujita, he noted that it was not unusual for the ninja to jump from heights of up to 50 feet on a regular basis. Fujita claimed that in later life he was able to leap from a height of up to 45 feet. Fujita explained that he used a furoshiki when he jumped from altitudes higher than 45 feet. He held the furoshiki with both hands and his teeth, forming a triangle shape that functioned like a parachute. According to Fujita, the ninja used the furoshiki in this way to jump from high altitudes in emergencies. Fujita claimed that this device was invented about 700 years ago to allow ninja to jump from castle walls. Other jumping techniques that Fujita mentioned involved planting hemp seed and using its rapid growth to drive the ninja's progress.[28]

Other techniques that Shintazaemon taught Fujita after he had become accustomed to the fundamental methods of walking on his toes and the outside of his feet were six practical or real methods of walking. They were designed to teach certain types of movement, rather than for simple conditioning. These techniques consisted of six methods of walking: forward, backward, sideways, broad walking, speed walking, and creeping. Unlike typical forward walking, the forward-moving technique involved rapid little steps that were executed with the ninja looking at his feet while he moved. Fujita explained that this technique, called "Rikitei,"[29] was designed to keep the ninja from tiring. Fujita believed this would happen if the ninja looked straight ahead, and therefore, the ninja would droop his head while moving. Fujita also claimed that a ninja was expected to be able to move 10 miles an hour, or 100 miles a day, and thus was required to undertake endurance training to acquire this ability. One such method involved putting a bamboo leaf on one's chest and reaching adequate speed to ensure that the leaf adhered to one's chest while moving. Another similar practice involved wearing a long, cloak-like cloth that would be worn around the ninja's neck while running, with the aim of attaining adequate speed so that the cloth would not touch the ground.

Fujita's training also included a technique that was used at night, called "Shako,"[30] which meant creeping. Fujita did not describe this method in detail, although he mentioned that it was the most important method of moving, as the enemy could still detect a ninja's shadow at night. Fujita also mentioned that a ninja might decide to feign disability, and at such times, he relied on combinations of the basic walking techniques mentioned above. An example Fujita gave was the possibility of walking on the tiptoes of one foot, while walking on the edge of the other, which would produce an awkward gait that closely resembled that of a physically handicapped person.[31]

In addition to physical techniques associated with the practice of the martial arts, Shintazaemon required Fujita to read Japanese and Chinese classics, learn world history, and practice Chinese calligraphy for two hours everyday, in between various types of physical exercises that he taught Fujita. At eight years of age, Fujita concentrated on practicing everyday.[32]

In March 1907, Fujita's father Morinosuke was called back to Tokyo to work with the Metropolitan Police, and the family moved back to the capital. While Fujita was sad to leave his mother's grave, he was nevertheless pleased to return to Tokyo.

One month later, Fujita was enrolled in elementary school, where he demonstrated that he was academically gifted. Fujita attributed his academic prowess to his experiences studying sutra at Daiji-dera and the scholarly aspects of Shintazaemon's training regimen. Once Fujita was enrolled in school, Shintazaemon would awaken him at 5:00 a.m. and make him practice ninjutsu for two hours each morning, before he went to school.[33]

Fujita records that he did not find school interesting, nor did he like the other students or his teachers. He saw them as snobbish, impertinent, and weak. Later in life he would reflect on his attitudes toward his classmates and concluded that he may have had an inferiority complex related to having been raised in the countryside around Itsuka-shi. Additionally, Fujita thought that he may have had social problems due to the recent loss of his mother.

All of these factors led Fujita to lash out against his peers, and he developed a habit of bullying his classmates. He also enjoyed shocking others, an example of which he recounted in his memoirs: One morning Fujita heard the bell for the morning assembly while he was playing on the second floor at school. He waited for a group of students to gather in the schoolyard below and then jumped from the second floor into their midst. He delighted in the shocked and surprised reactions of his peers.

Later, before the morning class began, his teacher called him and asked him: "Fujita, is it true that you jumped from the second floor?" "Yes," he answered. The teacher responded, "You should not do it. Use the stairs." "But, it's faster," he answered. "Stupid! Don't do it again!" the teacher demanded. "Why?" asked Fujita. "You may get injured," his teacher said. "I won't get injured," Fujita replied. "No, you were lucky today, but you will be hurt next time." "I will show you again," he insisted. "Don't do it again!" his teacher barked. Fujita was surprised at his teacher's lack of understanding and amazement at his abilities, a phenomenon that extended to his fellow students. And from that day forward, Fujita became a well-known student in the school.[34]

Fujita was very proud of his notoriety and increasingly resorted to his martial arts training as a means to impress and intimidate his classmates. Fujita would fight anyone he did not like, no matter how much bigger or older they were. When there was nobody left in school who was willing to fight him, Fujita went to another elementary school called Kuroda Kotoo, where most of the students were older than him. Fujita heard rumors of a student with a fearsome reputation named Kobayashi. One day, on his way home from school, Fujita went to Kuroda Kotoo with a group of followers and waited for Kobayashi. When the bell signaling the end of the school day rang and students emerged, one of Fujita's group pointed Kobayashi out, and Fujita walked directly into his path and stood and stared at him without saying a word. "Who are you?" Kobayashi demanded when he noticed Fujita staring at him. "I am Fujita. I have come here to fight you," Fujita answered. "OK, Come to Mount Renge," Kobayashi responded. Mount Renge was a place that was favored for fights between students of various local schools. Students normally engaged in a ritual that involved the students throwing their school colors, then proceeding to fight. In his fight with Kobayashi, Fujita records simply that he used his hands in the fight and he noted that he had an easy time defeating Kobayashi.[35]

Fujita was small, but he could strike more quickly than other people. He could strike four or five times in the time it took for his opponent to attempt just one strike. Fujita's fighting technique involved kicking his opponent's chin or closing in on his opponent and attacking head first, especially if his opponent was taller. He would then finish his opponent on the ground. Fujita further mentioned that he was able to beat even knife-wielding opponents, especially if he was able to use a stick, in combination with the jojutsu techniques he learned from the Yamabushi of Mount Mitsumine.[36]

When there was nobody left for him to fight in the nearby schools, Fujita started to pick fights with street gangsters. His father heard about his activities and warned him that he would get hurt if he continued to indulge his love of fighting. One day when Fujita was 13 years old, his father's prediction came true. Fujita received a letter of challenge from a person named Kimura Tatsuji, who was known as the most feared gang leader in the Yamanote area. In the letter Kimura challenged Fujita to appear at Mount Renge, unless he was too afraid, in which case the letter demanded that he cease to behave in an impertinent manner from then on.

Kimura was twenty-one years old at the time, and although his writing was very bad, the letter was sealed on the left side as was the custom for a letter of challenge. Fujita had beaten some of Kimura's followers in the past, and this was Kimura's attempt to avenge them. Fujita had heard that Kimura was reputed to have killed someone when he was only 10 years old, and Fujita concluded that fighting Kimura, unlike the other people he had fought, might require being willing to engage in a fight to the death. Fujita therefore hid a knife under his clothing and quietly left the house about an hour before the appointed time of the fight.

It was the time of the cherry blossoms, and they were all around as Fujita made his way to Mount Renge to fight Kimura. Mount Renge was not far from Fujita's house. It was about a 15-minute walk past Christian Hill, where he turned left at an abandoned church, and then right past the broken wall that surrounded the church. As Fujita was about to clear the stone wall, he felt someone close to him, and at that moment, he was stabbed in the right side of his stomach with a bamboo spear. Fujita lashed out in retaliation and, using the knife he had hidden in his clothing, slashed the shoulder of the man who attacked him.

The attacker then released the spear and rolled down the hill head first. Then the man got up and started running, followed closely by another man who was also fleeing in the same direction. Fujita believed that Kimura was his attacker and resolved to avenge his treachery. He removed the spear and pressed his right hand against the wound. Fujita then used his free left hand to remove his fundoshi, a traditional loincloth that is now rarely worn, and used it as a tourniquet. Although he didn't feel much pain, he felt dizzy from the massive blood loss from the wound he had received. It was already dark when Fujita began to make his way home, his legs dragging heavily because of his weakened state. When Fujita arrived home, he summoned all of his strength and snuck into his room via a nearby window. Fujita struggled onto his futon and covered himself with a blanket.

Fujita could not go to see a doctor, since he knew that his father would surely learn about his activities. Fujita reasoned that he had to keep his injury a secret, since he had already caused his father many problems in previous years. Fujita records that he snuck into his family kitchen and took a bottle of vinegar, which he used to wash his stomach wound, and he reapplied the makeshift tourniquet using his fundoshi.

Within three days, Fujita's wound had closed completely, and he acted as though nothing had happened. Fujita was furious with Kimura's breach of the accepted fighting protocol, which did not allow for ambushes, and he resolved to kill Kimura the next time he came across him. Fujita walked around searching for Kimura and his minions, but never found them. He later heard that the gang leader had fled, and Fujita believed that he had made a contribution to society by combating and dispersing this group of gangsters.[37]

FINAL LESSONS

In 1909, Shintazaemon became much stricter with the training of his grandson, and in retrospect, Fujita believed that Shintazaemon somehow knew that he would soon die, and he wanted to prepare Fujita to assume that mantle of inheritor of the Wada-ha Koga-ryu.[38] Fujita noted that ninjutsu techniques could not be learned by consulting ancient scrolls, for the scrolls only outlined the techniques; the lessons behind the techniques could only be passed on isshi shoden, from master to student. He also stated that one had to practice for many years to acquire the skills of the ninja, as is indicated by the root word "nin" of ninjutsu, which translates into patience.[39]

Among the techniques that Shintazaemon taught Fujita before he died were techniques that involved the strengthening of the internal organs, which Fujita claimed were part of ninjutsu asceticism. The first of these was "Mushu no Jutsu," a technique to stave off body odor. This technique allowed the ninja to hide in close proximity to his pursuers, without the fear that the exertions of his mission would reveal his position. "Mushu no Jutsu" involved abstaining from fishy foods, leaks, garlic, onions, and any other foods that had pungent or distinct smells. The ninja also forsook drinks that provoked heavy perspiration as part of "Mushu no Jutsu."[40]

Other techniques that Fujita mastered were fasting and sleep deprivation. He also practiced techniques that involved consuming huge amounts of food, by expanding and contracting his stomach. As a result he never felt sick, no matter how much he ate. Fujita claimed that this skill allowed the ninja to eat large amounts of food, in anticipation of going several days without it. Generally, the stomach is not considered a voluntary muscle, but Fujita insisted that it could be trained to come under conscious control, and he noted that he demonstrated this ability in public many times.

Although Fujita did not drink alcohol or smoke tobacco, he could indulge in these habits if necessary. Indeed, he believed that although he was not a regular drinker, he could will himself to remain sober, no matter how much alcohol he drank. Fujita also believed that he could condition his body to nicotine by smoking through his nose, which he claimed made it easier to absorb the nicotine into his stomach and lungs. He could also hold the smoke for long periods of time without breathing and could exhale it at will.

Fujita also noted that at one sitting, he could consume eight bowls of tendons. If he were eating soba noodles, he claimed he could eat 25 bowls of soba tendons, accompanied by 15 liters of alcohol, and 10 boxes of cigarettes, which, as mentioned before, he smoked through the nose for more rapid absorption of the nicotine.[41]

The last set of techniques that Fujita mentions learning from Shintazaemon involved methods of sharpening the five senses. He believed that one could enhance the effectiveness of his natural senses up to 14 times their normal capacity. According to Fujita the sense of sight could be increased up to eight times its normal capacity, and the senses of smell and taste could be increased up to three times their normal capacity. Fujita stated that by training in these methods, he could put his ear to the wall in any room, no matter how large, and be able to hear the conversation taking place on the opposite end of the room. Incredibly, he claimed that when he was in a meditative state, he could even hear ashes dropping from a cigarette.[42]

Fujita notes that his grandfather died on September 10, 1910, when Fujita was about 11 years old.[43] Fujita recorded that while Shintazaemon was on his deathbed, Shintazaemon called him over and gave him two volumes of scrolls related to the Wada-ha family of Koga ninjutsu. One of these scrolls may have been *Ninjutsu Hisho Ogiden no Kan* (The Secret Essence of Ninjutsu), which was written in 1544 and which details Koga ninja techniques. A photograph of this scroll appeared in Fujita's obituary when he died 56 years later.[44] Shintazaemon then passed on the mantle of Soke of the Wada-ha Koga-ryu to Fujita, saying: "The orthodox Koga-ryu will be ended after you."[45] After Shintazaemon's death, Fujita worked hard to complete his ninjutsu training so as not to disappoint his grandfather. He spent a lot of time perfecting his martial skills, working on them day and night, and gradually mastered ninjutsu.[46]

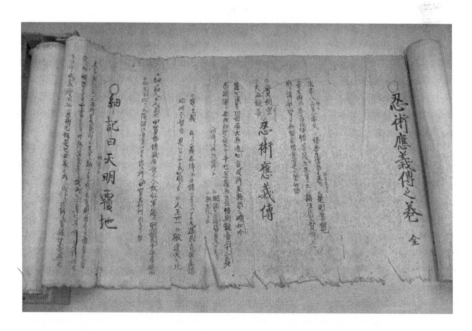

Ninjutsu Hisho Ogiden No Kan as it currently appears at Iga-Ueno Museum

THE YOUNG SEEKER

A year after his grandfather's death, Fujita, then 12 years old, left home with his father's permission to live once again with the Yamabushi. After spending two months with the Yamabushi, Fujita received transmission of two ascetic rituals: the *Kuji Goshin-Ho*, a rite of nine secret Buddhist hand (finger) patterns, and *Kuji Kiri*, a rite consisting of nine secret cuts or gestures, which are reputed to access paranormal abilities in esoteric Buddhism. Fujita went on to mention that these rituals opened up planes of consciousness that had formerly been unavailable to him. These included the ability to sense in which houses there would be a funeral, where an accident was imminent, and how to heal certain ailments. In addition to these abilities, Fujita also learned how to immobilize dangerous opponents via the rite of *Fudo Kanashibari*, a method of charming and immobilizing a subject.[47]

Fujita claimed that he was considered a child prodigy because of his strange abilities. He worked with a man named Tatashimaka Kiemon, who was well known in those days by those interested in the paranormal as a Shafuku, or medium. Fujita also claimed that a fortune teller named Keizo assisted in training him to see objects concealed in boxes or inserted in such places as the barrel of a gun.[48] The young master of the Wada-ha had become interested in paranormal phenomenon, and this spurred him to begin researching an array of subjects, including matters related to human souls, spirits, ghosts, and gods.

Fujita's interest in the paranormal was triggered by an experience that occurred before Shintazaemon died. Three months after his encounter with Kimura, and on the day of Obon (Buddhist All Souls' Day, held in July or August), while on his way home after looking for someone to fight, Fujita saw an old temple called Genkakuji. The temple was famous for wind-up dolls of Heaven and Hell, which, on festivals days like Obon, were shown by the monks of Genkakuji to entertain an audience that customarily gathered to see them perform. Fujita decided that he wanted to see the dolls, too, so he made his way through the crowd to the front of the line. In the fading sunlight of evening stood statues of Emma, flanked by a red demon and blue demon, casting dead bodies into mortar stones to be ground up. To add to this scene, the monks had lit incense and chanted a song that caught the young Fujita's ear:

"People who commit evil deeds while they are alive will either sink into a bloody pond, or be forced to climb a mountain in Hell that is full of needles. Their bodies will then be destroyed in a stone mortar. A red demon and blue demon show no mercy."[49]

These simple words struck a chord with Fujita, as did the peculiar movement of the dolls, which were pulled into motion by the monks, using ropes attached to the dolls like marionettes. The peculiar nature of the dolls' movement made them all the more frightening, and Fujita found it unbearable to look at them. He thought about turning away and heading home, but his innate defiance inspired him to conclude that the song was a lie. This angered Fujita, who picked up a large rock, which he hurled in the direction of the closest doll. There followed a loud crash as the doll collapsed, causing the surprised crowd to recoil in shock and the monks to hurl themselves into the crowd in Fujita's direction. He ducked behind a group of nearby people but was quickly identified by members of the crowd:

"That's him."

"He's over there!"

"Catch him!"

Fujita's heart was beating furiously, and he fled the temple with a few monks and temple students following him.

A monk screamed "Wait! I'll beat you to death!"[50]

Fujita continued running through the alleys, toward the train station, to the South Hill, Kasuga-shi, across a field and another hill, and still the monks continued their relentless pursuit. Fujita was amazed by their determination, and time after time, he turned back to see if the monks had broken off their pursuit. The monks, in fact, had not, because they intended to avenge the destruction of the temple treasure. They chased Fujita for about an hour, but he knew the small paths near his home better than they did, and when finally he had escaped his determined pursuers, he was overcome by exhaustion.

That night, Fujita ran a fever and could not escape replaying the day's events and the monks' song: "People who commit evil deeds . . ." He heard it in his mind, and when he slept, he dreamt that the red demon and blue demon appeared and seized him, putting him in the stone mortar, which shocked him out of his sleep, screaming. When his stepmother woke him, he was covered in sweat. He changed and went back to sleep, only to have the same nightmare. He was unable to go back to sleep because he feared that Emma was waiting for him in his dreams with the song that had scared him at the temple earlier that day.

For three nights the same dream revisited Fujita, leading to insomnia and weight loss due to his fear. During the following days and nights, his thoughts were consumed with the question as to whether or not hell existed. Four days later, a monk visited Fujita's home for an Obon memorial service, and Fujita's plight moved him to ask the monk whether or not hell existed, since he believed the monk would know. So he asked: "Is there a Hell after life?"

The monk replied: "Yes, there is."

Fujita retorted: "It's a lie."

The monk responded: "It's not a lie. A mischievous person like you is forced to stand in front of a mirror called 'the mirror of Shouma' and see all the bad things that he has done in the past. Then, the person will be thrown into a stone mortar and ground by a red demon and a blue demon, using a pestle."[51]

Fujita was silent in response to these comments by the monk, since they were exactly the same as the story he had heard at the temple. Fujita became convinced that he would suffer at the hands of Emma and his demons after he died. His every thought was that of Heaven and Hell.

The entire series of events that began when Fujita passed the temple by chance some days earlier had led him to become consumed with fear and curiosity about what happened to the human soul after death. After he failed to receive comfort from the answers of the various monks to whom he had spoken, Fujita approached the two men on whom he had depended since birth for sustenance and knowledge: his father and grandfather. When Fujita asked his grandfather as to whether there was a real Hell, Shintazaemon's answer was short and exactly what Fujita did not want to hear: "There is." His father Morinosuke, on the other hand, was more modern and philosophical in his response: "I cannot say there is or is not."[52] Whatever Fujita may have thought of these responses at the time, we do know that his interest in the human soul and other paranormal phenomena developed from an interest motivated by fear and self-preservation. This initial impetus evolved into a lifelong search into the many practices that allowed access to the strange realm of paranormal powers.

Fujita's interest in the paranormal made him very much a man of his time. As Japan was modernizing at the end of the Meiji era, many of the nation's intellectuals were becoming interested in both traditional magical practices and new ideas related to the paranormal. These included practices such as hypnotism and psychic research, which were popular around the world during the first decade of the 20th century.

The popularity of these topics at the end of the Meiji era spawned numerous famous researchers and organizations related to these fields. Among these were Yamaguchi Sannosuke from Teikoku Saimin Gakkai (Teikoku Hypnotism Association), and Hukukei Ono of the Dai Nippon Saiminjutsu Shourei Kai (Japan Hypnotism Association). Others in whom Fujita was interested included Dr. Hukurai Tomokichi, who earned a degree in psychic studies and conducted extensive research related to these phenomena. Fujita also paid attention to the activities of Dr. Inoue Enryo, who was nicknamed the "Doctor of Ghosts." Because of the popularity of this genre of studies, there was an abundance of books related to paranormal subjects. They included both academic and non-academic publications, and Fujita voraciously read them all, in an attempt to expand his knowledge.[53]

For all of his interest in the paranormal, Fujita claimed his supposed abilities were not miraculous. Fujita made the following statement about paranormal phenomenon: "With practice, anyone could put their hand in boiling water, or walk barefoot through fire, etc. From the start I recognized that jutsu (art or practice) is not a miracle. The point is practice."[54] What is beyond dispute is that Fujita was able to perform many physical feats that would be considered beyond the normal range of accepted human behavior, with his pain tolerance being the most commonly recorded and photographed. This ability to tolerate pain was such that it impressed even the most hardened of his martial arts contemporaries.[55]

Later in his life Fujita would admit that his interest in topics related to the paranormal had led him to behave and dress in an eccentric manner in his early adult years. This eccentricity also stemmed from his previously mentioned vocation as a Shafuku and fortune teller and his involvement in fringe religious organizations that were outside the mainstream of Japanese society. Fujita's eccentricities would later be used by some of his critics as fodder for condemning all of his works in other areas of his life, such as his martial arts practice and his writings.

THE FORMATIVE YEARS

In the years between 1910, when his grandfather Shintazaemon died, and 1919, when he graduated from Nippon University with a degree in religious studies, Fujita was exposed to many experiences and practices that would set him on his career path for the rest of his life.

After graduating from Soujitsu in 1914, which he had attended after leaving elementary school, Fujita enrolled in a series of universities: Waseda, Tokyo, and Meiji—all of which expelled him for his customary inclination toward fighting. During his series of university enrollments, he embarked on his writing career, working as a journalist for newspaper companies such as *Houchi, The Hibi, The Yamato, The Kokumin,* and *The Chugai.*[56] This delving into the arena of journalism would eventually develop into a prolific career that produced numerous newspaper and research articles and over half a dozen books related to the martial arts.

In addition to his journalistic activities, Fujita also taught judo and kendo, which he had learned during his school years, at the Tokyo Metropolitan Police Department, where his father Morinosuke had served until 1912. After his graduation from Nippon University, Fujita held teaching positions at *The Toyoma School, The Rikudai* (The University of the Army) and *The Kaidai* (The University of the Navy).[57]

Yet even with his new intellectual pursuits, Fujita still had not lost his penchant for getting himself into trouble, and a particular incident involving a Yakuza (Japanese underworld) member illustrates this.

A member of the Yakuza had heard of Fujita's reputation as a feared fighter and tendered a challenge to Fujita. Fujita arranged a meeting in a restaurant and brought along a journalist friend of his. The journalist recounts the following story:

> "We were, all three of us, sitting at the table, when the waitress came to take our order. 'I want red meat, very rare,' said the Yakuza man in a belligerent tone of voice. Fujita replied to the waitress: 'Bring only sake and boiling water (to cook the meat, as for fondue)' then, drawing his pocket knife, he cut from his own thigh a piece of flesh three centimeters thick, plunged it into the boiling water for a few seconds, then deposited it on the

Yakuza's plate. He then poured alcohol on the wound to disinfect it and made a compress out of his own scarf to stop the bleeding, all of this without saying a word. The Yakuza, his eyes wide, realized that he was not dealing with a normal individual, and left the table, without saying a word."[58]

Along with his new interests in teaching academic subjects, teaching judo and kendo, and journalistic writing, Fujita continued to add to his repertoire of traditional bujutsu. Between the ages of 13 and 18 years, he learned a version of the bugei juhappan, or 18 warrior strategies. Fujita learned most of these from his father and his grandfather. Fujita's version of the bugei juhappan consisted of numerous diverse martial arts traditions and practices:

Fujita's Bugei Juhappan		
Iaijutsu (art of drawing the sword)	Kusarijutsu (chains)	Kusarigama (sickle and chain)
Daien Ryu Bojutsu (school of the long staff of the Great Circle)	Shurikenjutsu of Shingetsu-ryu (thrown weapons of the school of the New Moon)	Heiho (military strategy)
Jojutsu (Shinto Musu-ryu)	Ichiden-ryu Torite (restraining techniques)	Tenmon (psychological sciences related to espionage)
Kenjutsu (the sword style of Muso shinden-ryu)	Yawara (jujutsu or unarmed combat)	Towatejutsu (hand weapons and diversions)
Yarijutsu (spear)	Suihejutsu (different forms of swimming, armored and without)	Kayakujutsu (handling of explosives)
Naginatajutsu (halberd)	Yumi (archery)	Hinawajutsu (firearms)[59]

It was also during these years that Fujita came into contact with a mysterious and obscure martial art known as Nanban Satto-ryu Kempo. This martial art, which has often been mentioned in connection with Fujita's name and in combination with the mystique surrounding his ninjutsu, has often been the subject of rampant speculation and misidentification.

NANBAN SATTO RYU KEMPO

Nanban Satto-ryu Kempo can be translated as "Southern Barbarian Swarm Upon Fist Method." A translation of the individual words is as follows: "Nanban" means "barbarian south" and is used to refer to countries near Japan (i.e., China). "Satto" means to "swarm upon," or "come down on," and is a term commonly used in the Japanese language. The term "kempo," which means "fist way" or "fist method," is just the Japanese way of reading the Chinese chuang fa. However, the fact that some schools use the term *kempo* does not by definition mean they are of Chinese origin.[60] Contrary to popular thought in the West, kempo does not necessarily suggest a system in the Okinawan karate vein of kicking and punching; it also includes traditional Japanese arts that, to varying degrees, include striking, throwing, and locking techniques, which are included today under the umbrella name of jujutsu.

When Fujita was about 15 years old, he had an encounter with this martial art, Nanban Satto-ryu Kempo, which would become almost as inextricably linked to him as ninjutsu is today. Fujita described his initial experience with the art as follows:

"One day, as I was going round a corner, I heard the noises of people training, but I couldn't see a sign directing me to a dojo entrance. Finally, I found the place from which the sounds were emanating, and entered into a hall, where there were several people and a frail old man, who seemed as though he could have been easily snuffed out, like a candle. Before I could say a word, the old man said to me: 'You have come here to fight; that is good; come, approach me.' He had a white beard that hung all the way down to his solar plexus. When the fight began, the attitude of the individual before me was no longer that of an old man, but that of a wild cat. He feinted and countered all my attacks; I had the impression that he was playing with me, like a cat with a mouse.

Contraried, I decided no longer to take into consideration the age of this venerable grandfather and to attack with more sincerity. I could see the man's eyes transform into a torrent of fire and, without my being able to do a thing, he touched me with the tips of his fingers with lightening speed, and I lost consciousness. This man's name was Hashimoto Ippussai.

He was the second patriarch of the Nanban Satto Ryu Kempo. When I regained consciousness, the man told me: 'Victory is not obtained through physical force alone;' then he introduced himself and I reciprocated. One of the particular points of the Nanban Satto Ryu Kempo (school) is work done with the tips of the fingers and toes, to perforate the enemy, as one could with a saber or a steel spear. All the strikes in this school are directed against pressure points on the human body. For five years, I trained hard in the art of kempo."[61]

Fujita had additional recollections about Hashimoto's prowess and stated the following: "He could break the bamboo pipes used for flower arrangement with the tips of his flexible fingers. Even though my fingers have a diameter of 1 sun (3.03cm) and are about 1 ishhaku (30cm) long, if I bind all four together and try to use my whole hand to break one, I still can't."[62]

For Fujita, his encounter with Nanban Satto-ryu Kempo was an introduction to what would become the overt manifestation of his martial arts during his lifetime. While his reputation is based on his claim to have been the "last ninja," jujutsu, specifically Nanban Satto-ryu Kempo, was what Fujita most often taught and demonstrated. Like his Wada-ha Koga-ryu, Nanban Satto-ryu Kempo would be a central part of many mistaken stories and theories relating to Fujita's legacy in the decades following his death. Contrary to the commonly accepted view of Nanban Satto-ryu Kempo in the West today, which is defined by the presence of the word kempo in its title, and the conclusion that it is akin to the Okinawan art of the same name, the facts about this art are quite different.

In the *Bugei Ryuha Daijiten*, Nanban Satto-ryu Kempo is listed as being related to an obscure art called Nanban Ippo-ryu Jujutsu, which was founded at the end of the Edo period by Hashimoto Ippusai, a samurai from the Satsuma province. Nanban Ippo-ryu jujutsu is said to be based on the Toritejutsu (jujutsu) of Nobeoka-han, in what used to be the Hyuga province during the Sengoku period (warring states). During this period, the southern half of Hyuga was part of the domain of the Shimazu clan, which ruled the neighboring Satsuma province. Also listed on the same page of the *Bugei Ryuha Daijiten* is a lineage for Nanban Satto-ryu Kempo, which begins with the founder of the art, Hashimoto Ippusai (1), who passed it on to a son or grandson of the same name, Hashimoto Ippusai (2), the man whom the 15-year-old Fujita encountered on that fateful day when he discovered the art. Fujita is then listed as the 3rd Soke, inheriting the art in 1919. Also recorded as receiving menkyo kaiden in the same generation as Fujita was Miura Hayato Takaren, who added the Hojojutsu of Naegi-han to his school and called it "Nanban-ryu." Miura is also listed as eventually passing Nanban-ryu on to a student named Uchida Shichirobei Takayasu. There is an additional entry relating to Nanban Satto-ryu Kempo, which mentions Fujita's chosen inheritor, Iwata Manzo, a famous practitioner of Shito-ryu Karate, as succeeding Fujita in 1948, as the 4th Soke of the system.[63]

Nanban Satto-ryu densho

According to a description of the art found in the brochure of the Nihon Kobudo Shinkokai, Nanban Satto-ryu Kempo is described as follows: "The art teaches how to successfully combine striking (atemi), throwing techniques (nage waza), and locking techniques (Kansetsu waza), while encouraging the flexibility to adapt freely to an infinite number of applications. As such, many techniques are dangerous, and are passed down from headmaster to headmaster only (isshi shoden)."[64] Additional substance is given to the claim that Nanban Satto-ryu Kempo was intended for real fighting, since the same source says the following about the founder of the art: "A warrior from Satsuma, Hashimoto Ippusai is the founder (Kaiso). He used this art actively during the battle of Toba Fushimi (1868; Kyoto)."[65]

Another mistaken interpretation that often runs parallel to the idea that Nanban Satto-ryu Kempo is akin to Okinawan arts of the same name, is that Nanban Satto-ryu Kempo is related to Fujita's Wada-ha Koga-ryu Ninjutsu. Some people have attempted to connect Wada-ha Koga-ryu and Nanban Satto-ryu Kempo and used this incorrect connection to arrive at the equally incorrect conclusion that ninjutsu is related to arts similar to Okinawan arts of the same name.

The following hypothesis illustrates the attempts to tie together the histories of ninjutsu and the Okinawan martial art of kempo. Indeed, the error is such that it not only attempts to make the case for a connection between the three mentioned arts but actually mistakenly combines the names of Wada-ha Koga-ryu and Nanban Satto-ryu Kempo, somehow arriving at the name "Koga Ha Sato Ryu." The following is a quote that illustrates this situation:

> "Two other men should be noted, one may be unknown in America, and the other unsung in the ninjutsu tradition. First there is Seiko Fujita, who as noted above was one of the truly great historians of the martial arts. He was also the headmaster of 'Koga Ha Sato Ryu.' He was as such an accomplished master of ninjutsu and kempo. It is said that he instructed his students to study not only the traditional Japanese arts but to explore the Okinawan arts as well, having them study karate and Ryukyu kobujutsu. There is a special connection between Okinawan martial arts and ninjutsu which will be explored later."[66]

Additional claims have also been made that Fujita, who during his life studied with numerous martial artists both Japanese and Okinawan, had met, while studying with the legendary Okinawan master Motobu Choki, James Masayoshi Mitose, the famous Japanese-American who is considered to be the father of "American Kenpo." This hypothesis suggests that Fujita taught Mitose both ninjutsu and Nanban Satto Ryu Kempo, as illustrated by the following quote:

> "If it is true that Mitose studied Koga Ryu Ninjutsu, from whom did he learn it? A Japanese ninjutsu master living in Canada verifies the fact that Seiko Fujita did in fact teach Koga Ryu Ninjutsu and that Mitose studied with him during his time in Japan. This makes perfect sense, since Fujita was part of the entourage that trained with Motobu. It is believed then that Mitose trained in kempo karate (known variously as Motobu Ryu, Shuri Ryu, and Shorei Ryu) and ninjutsu, specifically Koga Ryu, and possibly the related Sato Ryu Kempo, which was also taught by Seiko Fujita. There has always been a close relation between kempo and ninjutsu, mainly through the temples where kempo developed and the ninpo concept of patience as a religious discipline and its application to espionage."[67]

Unfortunately for those who espouse this theory, there is no evidence to corroborate this claim. Fujita, a meticulous documenter of his peers' and students' names, never mentions Mitose. In addition, those to whom Fujita taught Nanban Satto-ryu Kempo are well known, with their names documented in various places, including the *Bugei Ryuha Diajiten*, Mitose is not among those documented. The fact that the claim is supposedly substantiated by quoting a ninjutsu master living in Canada also brings the claim into question, since Japanese martial arts authorities accept only two sources as existing at the time: Fujita himself, and Takamatsu Toshitsugu, the teacher of Hatsumi Masaaki, who would later go on to popularize ninjutsu, decades after Mitose supposedly studied with Fujita. There also does not appear to be any evidence that Mitose himself ever made this claim. In his two books related to his version of the art of kempo: *What Is Self Defense?* (Kenpo Jiu-Jitsu) (1953), and *In Search Of Kenpo* (1984), no claim of any connection to Fujita exists. In fact, all claims that Mitose's kempo contains components of Wada-ha Koga-ryu and Nanban Satto-ryu Kempo are discredited by the clear Okinawan derivation of Mitose's kempo skills.

Another famous Japanese martial artist and contemporary of Fujita's was Konishi Yasuhiro, founder of Shindo Jinen-ryu Karate-jutsu and a fellow student of Motobu's, who later studied Nanban Satto-ryu Kempo with Fujita. Konishi was originally a practitioner of jujutsu and kendo and later went on to become a famous karate pioneer. He trained with Motobu at the same time as Fujita and recollects the interesting cast of characters that surrounded Motobu:

"Konishi remembered the original group of Motobu's karate students
in Tokyo. It included such people as Seiko Fujita, a jujutsu and martial arts
expert who is remembered in some quarters as the 'last officially recognized
Ninja' (i.e., the last to see active service), Lion Kamemitsu, a Sumo Wrestler,
and Piston Horiguchi, a boxer—and a colorful group it must have been."[68]
Yet again, Mitose's name is conspicuously absent.

Indeed, no less a figure than Motobu's own son, Motobu Chosei, insists that Mitose
never trained with his father, since Motobu Choki never mentioned him as being among
his list of original students.[69] Those advocating the Fujita-Mitose connection may simply
chalk all of this up to oversight on the part of Konishi and Motobu; however, this too
seems improbable in the extreme. If Fujita had taught Mitose his two most mysterious
arts, Mitose would surely have had to be an exceptional and memorable figure. These
are precisely the characteristics that would have been sought out by Konishi, who is
known as a voracious acquirer of martial skills. This fact is attested to by Konishi's
array of teachers: Funakoski Gichin, founder of Shotokan; Motobu Choki; Mabuni
Kenwa, founder of Shito-ryu Karate-do; and Ueshiba Morihei, founder of Aikido; and,
of course, Fujita.

All of those who learned Nanban Satto-ryu Kempo from Fujita are well known and
can demonstrate a clear connection to him. We know from earlier mentions of him that
Iwata Manzo succeeded Fujita as Yondai (4th) Soke in 1948, but he was not the only
person to whom Fujita taught Nanban Satto-ryu Kempo, since we have already singled
out Konishi. Another man who will be discussed later is Inoue Motokatsu, a lifelong
student of Fujita's. There is also Ueno Takahashi, a famous koryu bujutsu master and
inheritor of numerous arts. Ueno was taught Nanban Satto-ryu Kempo in exchange
for teaching Fujita ShintoTenshin-ryu Kempo.[70] There are two additional claims of
inheritance of Nanban Satto-ryu Kempo from Fujita that involve his two sons-in-law.
The first is a persistent claim that Fujita taught Nanban Satto-ryu Kempo to his son-
in-law, Ueda Isamu, at the request of his daughter, Ueda Yuku, a claim that cannot be
officially verified, since no documentation is publically available. The second is a claim
by a well-known French martial artist and writer, Sylvain Guintard, that he was issued
Gokui Menkyo Kaiden in Nanban Satto-ryu Kempo by Fujita's other son-in-law, Yoshi,
who took the name Fujita, to honor his famous father-in-law.[71]

Today, Nanban Satto-ryu Kempo remains alive among a few select practitioners
who were students of Iwata Manzo. The most important of these is Iwata's son, Iwata
Genzo, who is listed as succeeding Iwata Manzo as Godai (5th) Soke.[72] Iwata Manzo
also taught Nanban Satto-ryu Kempo to his uchi-deshi (live-in disciple), Murayama
Kunio. Murayama had started training under Iwata at Toyo University, where he rose
to become captain of the Toyo University Karate Team, from 1966 to 1968. Murayama
was then selected to live in Iwata's home as his uchi-deshi between 1968 and 1970,
since he was being groomed to get his teaching license in Shito-ryu Karate. Murayama
recalls that he would practice for hours each day, in the private Iwata family dojo, and

that Shito-ryu Karate and Nanban Satto-ryu Kempo were the main focus, although he was also trained in Daien-ryu Jojutsu and Shingetsu-ryu Shurikenjutsu.[73]

At present, Iwata Genzo is focusing on the teaching of Shito-ryu Karate, the art for which his father was most well known, and for which he currently performs the duty of head instructor at the art's Honbu Dojo. In response to a request for information about his father, Iwata Genzo wrote the following to Sam Moledzki, a high-ranking Canadian student of Murayama. "Satto-ryu Kempo, its techniques have no name, only within Bunkai Kumite (real applications) practice (Shito-ryu), this part is Satto-ryu. This is the way I was taught. Bunkai Kumite was taught by Mabuni Kenwa but some parts were changed (by Iwata Manzo) for Satto-ryu style."[74]

So today, with rare exceptions that sometimes arise in seminars held by Murayama, the Bunkai Kumite of the Shito-Kai branch of the Shito-ryu Karate presents the best opportunity to witness glimpses of the techniques of Nanban Satto-ryu Kempo. For those interested in the traditional Japanese martial arts, and more particularly those interested in the facts of Fujita's career, it can only be hoped that Nanban Satto-ryu Kempo will defy the fate of so many pre-Meiji era Japanese martial arts and live on through the 21st century and beyond.

THE WAR YEARS

One of the greatest areas of mystery and contention in Fujita's career is the matter of his wartime activities. In the West, with the advent of the ninja boom of the 1980s, fantastic rumors of Fujita's supposed exploits during the war spread. One of the more popular stories is attributed by some to Fujita's student, Inoue Motokatsu. It is claimed that Fujita led a special operations ninja unit of 50 men, who were tasked with battling British sabotage efforts in Burma, which began after the Japanese occupied the British colony. According to this story, supposedly attributed to Inoue, who is alleged to have been a member of the unit, the focus of Fujita's operation was the strategic Tamarkan Bridge. It is further claimed that Fujita's unit did not carry any conventional weapons and used only traditional ninjutsu tools. This story goes on to claim that Fujita's ninja unit operated in Burma from July 1941, before the outbreak of hostilities between Britain and Japan, and stayed there until May 1944, when 17 men left in the unit were evacuated to Japan. Among the survivors were Inoue and Fujita himself, who is credited with having personally killed 200 men while in Burma.[75]

In fact, the actual details of Fujita's wartime service, as documented in the various sources that have come down to us today, are far less glamorous than the claims made about him in the West. As has already been mentioned, Fujita held teaching positions at the *Rikudai* and *Kaidai*.

We also know from his writings that Fujita was appointed to a teaching position at the famed Nakano Spy School in 1937 and that he supposedly participated in some unspecified reconnaissance missions for the Japanese military, which could possibly be those described in the alleged Burma operation.[76] While we do not have documentary evidence to substantiate these claims, we do have evidence that Fujita was focused on studying the relationship between the historical ninja and modern espionage during the war years, as evidenced by the 1942 publication of Fujita's book, *Ninjutsu kara Supai Sen-e* (From Ninjutsu to Spy Warfare). Fujita relays to us that he attempted to teach certain aspects of his Wada-ha Koga-ryu to some of his students at the Nakano School but that his efforts failed because of the time factor. The Japanese military needed operatives who could be rapidly trained and sent to the various battle fronts. This demand for rapid results precluded the possibility of efficiently learning and using the skills of the ninja, which require far greater investments of time than do more conventional systems of training special operations personnel.

Nonetheless, anecdotal evidence suggests that philosophical ideas more akin to those of the ninja rather than the samurai prevailed among those trained by the Nakano organization. In an unprecedented directive, Nakano graduates were forbidden from indulging the prevailing philosophy of the Japanese military, which held that death was preferable to the dishonor of surrender or capture. An account of this divergence with the rest of the Japanese military's philosophy comes to us from the records of the Futumata Branch of the Nakano School which state the following: "Another point that Kumagawa and his staff drilled into their students was that each was to stay alive to accomplish his mission. The instruction was at odds with the prevailing ethos of the Japanese Army that called for an honorable death before the 'dishonor' of surrender. Japanese military leaders based this precept on a Japanese martial tradition that held that the way of the warrior was the way of death."[77] Additional support for the fact that the Nakano warriors were influenced by a philosophy other than the samurai ethos of the way of the warrior comes to us from the recollections of a man who is arguably the Nakano School's most famous graduate, Onoda Hiro.

Onoda was trained at the Futumata Branch in 1944 and was promptly sent to the Philippines to conduct guerilla operations against the Americans in support of the beleaguered Japanese occupation force. Onoda, who some have claimed was instructed by Fujita while he was a cadet at the Nakano school, recounted the following related to the orders given to his unit in the Philippines: "For Japan's shadow warriors, staying alive at all costs was imperative, no matter how great the shame of having other Japanese regard one as a traitor or coward. In the event that escape proved impossible at some point in the future, Onoda was to surrender rather than kill himself. In death, he was useless to Japan. As a prisoner, he could still serve by feeding his captors bogus intelligence."[78]

Indeed, other aspects of the training of the Nakano School during Fujita's tenure as an instructor from 1937 onward suggest that the ninja, rather than the samurai, were the philosophical inspiration for the training of cadets like Onoda. In addition to the prohibition against suicide to avoid capture, cadets at the school were also encouraged to hold opinions that were critical of everything, including the emperor. This aspect of their training was designed to encourage the critical thinking and individualism necessary for intelligence and guerilla training. This again was starkly at odds with the prevailing ethos and suggests that the ninja, and individuals like Fujita, were the influence: "Much of the training at the Futumata Branch struck Onoda as similar to that of Japan's fabled ninja. In fact, he and his classmates practiced such traditional stealth techniques as walking up against a wall to avoid casting a shadow."[79]

Whatever the inspiration for the training, Onoda learned it well, for while the Japanese war effort was doomed, Onoda not only resisted the urge to commit suicide, but he also continued to resist the Americans long after all other resistance ended. Despite numerous efforts by the Americans, and later the Filipinos, Onoda managed to evade them, all the while subsisting on whatever he could gather from the jungle, escaping capture until he was finally talked out of the jungle by a Japanese journalist in 1975, more than 30 years after being sent there on his fateful mission. Onoda's feat was so extraordinary that upon his emergence from the Lubang jungle of the Philippines in 1975, he became an instant sensation among the Japanese public, including those interested in the lore of the ninja: "It is amazing that he could have survived for twenty-nine years in the Philippine jungle, seven years of which he was entirely alone. One could argue that Onoda was the last ninja."[80]

Additional information that some claim sheds light on Fujita's wartime activities comes to us in the preface written by Fujita for his book, *Kempo Gokui Atemi No Sakkatsu-Ho Meikai* (Illustrated Secret Kempo Killing Strikes). The book, which was published in 1958, deals with the secret methodology of attacking pressure points, with the aim of causing injury or death. The book was later translated by the French martial arts pioneer, Henry Plee. The translation of Fujita's book was then published in 1998 under the title, *L'Art Sublime et Ultime des Points Vitaux* (The Sublime and Ultimate Art of Vital Points). In the translation, Plee claims that the preface was actually written in 1944. According to Plee, Fujita, because of his reputation as a skilled martial artist, was tasked by the Japanese government to arrive at a methodology that would give Japanese soldiers and sailors an advantage in the brutal hand-to-hand combat that was taking place in the Pacific. Plee claims that the initial impetus for the experiments undertaken by Fujita took place in Japanese-occupied China, when the Japanese military interrogated Chinese martial artists to extract information from them that might be useful to Japan's war effort. Plee then claims that between 1943 and 1944, the Nihon Bujutsu Kenkyu Jo (Japanese National Research Center for the Ancestral Warrior Techniques) held conferences with the heads of Japan's traditional martial arts systems to determine the effectiveness of pressure point attacks, with special emphasis on those that brought immediate results, such as incapacitation or death. It is claimed that thirty-four traditional Japanese ryuha (schools) contributed portions of their densho (scrolls) to this effort and that these schools appear in both Fujita's original work and Plee's translation. Plee further suggests that Fujita used Allied prisoners-of-war as the subjects of his experiments that ultimately resulted in the new methodology, with particular emphasis on the differences in reaction between subjects of African and European ancestry on the one hand and Asians on the other.[81] Plee then offers what he claims is a quote from the original study, which details the methodology of the supposed experiments, but he unfortunately does not reference any verifiable document as the source of the quote other than to say that it was part of a "top secret" report that he had the good fortune to see.[82]

The quote in Plee's book is as follows: "The prisoner is struck in such way at the vital point X, the prisoner collapses, and is reanimated with such kuatsu. It is struck anew with a greater power, the heart stops, and nevertheless is reanimated after X minutes with such other kuatsu, has such vital point [struck] the heart stops, but this time is not reanimated, and so on."[83]

Plee then goes on to reference Fujita's preface, which appears at the beginning of *Kempo Gokui Atemi No Sakkatsu-Ho Meikai* to substantiate his claims:

> "This work includes a complete physical and physiological study of documents provided by the ryu (Ancient martial art schools) of Japan with regard to the Kyusho, Gokui and Satsu-kappo. It contains the conclusions of the studies made by the Japanese National Research Center on the Ancestral Warrior Techniques (Nihon Bujutsu Kenkyu Jo) with regard to the authenticity of the vital points of the human body and ancestral methods of reanimation.
>
> It gives the precise anatomical references and the scientific explanations making it possible to cause internal injuries which have immediate or delayed effect. The conclusions have been made on the basis of experiments, very many having caused the unconsciousness as well as the death of the experimental subjects.
>
> If the vital points mentioned are touched or struck according to instructions given, and if one executes the methods of reanimation such as are described, one will obtain the result exactly as indicated.
>
> My sincere wish that all who are devoted to the study of this work proceed with the most total confidence.
>
> FUJITA SEIKO, 10th dan
> 14th Patriarch of Koga-ryu Ninjutsu and Satto-ryu Kempo
> Chief of the Japanese National Research Center on the Ancestral Warrior Techniques (Nihon Bujutsu Kenkyu Jo) "[84]

According to Plee, Fujita's preface is the first page of a "top secret" report submitted to instructors of Japanese special operations units tasked with forming guerilla units constituted to resist American forces in the Pacific theater of operations. A review of the preface certainly does raise some interesting questions, namely, how literally should the mention of experiments be taken? And what environment and circumstances, other than the war, could allow for experiments that resulted in unconsciousness and death? Indeed, there are documented incidents of Japanese servicemen using methods similar to those seemingly advocated in Fujita's preface. Interestingly, one incident involves war crimes committed by some of the same men whom Fujita may have been involved in training when they were cadets at the Nakano School. One such incident that took place during the last days of the war is described as follows: "On the evening of 10 August (1945) Captain Itezano Tatsuo called a meeting of around twenty shadow warriors engaged in guerilla training. He informed them that, on orders of senior air staff officer Colonel Sato Yoshinao, all officers involved in guerilla warfare were to participate the next morning in the execution of eight American prisoners. Itezano further informed them that karate and arrows would be used. Lieutenant Yamamoto Fukuichi remarked how he wished to test his skill in karate on a prisoner. Itezano had secured permission from Sato to apply his unit's guerilla training on the prisoners as a form of live exercise."[85]

In the interest of a balanced review of the preface and the theory that it was based on experiments using captured Allied servicemen, it must be said that the preface is only suggestive and certainly not definitive. While the history of the war in the Pacific, and specifically that of the Nakano School, to which Fujita was attached as an instructor, does reveal atrocities against prisoners of war using martial arts skills, the preface itself contains neither a description of the supposed subjects of the vital point experiments, nor the circumstances under which they were conducted.

In fact, the organization under which the alleged experiments were conducted, the Nihon Bujutsu Kenkyu Jo, is reputed by most martial arts scholars as having been founded in 1951, six years after the war ended. According to this claim, the organization was founded to compile information about, and to preserve, Japanese martial arts, after these arts had been banned by Allied occupation authorities at the war's end. Plee's theory would suggest that either the accepted facts as to the founding of the Nihon Bujutsu Kenkyu Jo are incorrect or the preface to Plee's translation of Fujita's *Kempo Gokui Atemi No Sakkatsu-Ho Meikai* was written well after the 1944 date claimed by Plee.

There is also the possibility that Fujita may be simply restating the experiences of the various Japanese ryuha, collected by the Nihon Bujutsu Kenkyu Jo in its capacity as a preservation society, when he recommends the methods documented in *Kempo Gokui Atemi No Sakkatsu-Ho Meikai*. This would certainly explain why there is no specific mention of experiments on Allied prisoners. Some who have researched the matter of Fujita's reputed experiments and guerilla activities during the war have concluded that the fact that Fujita was not charged with any atrocities after the war is proof that his role was far less substantial than Plee and others claim. One such researcher says the following about Fujita's wartime activities: "His [Fujita's] biggest contribution to the war effort was to teach sections of strategy taken from the *Bansenshukai* at some of the military academies. On the day the war ended he was still safe in Japan."[86]

In truth, the facts of Fujita's role in the Japanese war effort are as mysterious and intriguing as much of the rest of his career. What he himself documented is interesting but scant, and his reputation, as it relates to ninjutsu, invites distortion both because of the passage of time and the sometimes deliberate fabrications of those interested in benefiting by claiming connection to Fujita's career.

What can be said with absolute certainty is that Fujita himself did claim to have taught at the Nakano School and several other military academies and to have carried out several unspecified reconnaissance missions for the Japanese government. That being said, the evidence does tend to suggest, though it does not prove, that Fujita was very influential in the development and teaching of the Nakano curriculum, insofar as it was influenced by the art and lore of the ninja. It must be noted, however, that Fujita's name does not appear among the names of the instructors documented in Stephen C. Mercado's *The Shadow Warriors of Nakano*, the seminal work on the topic of the Nakano School, in the English language.

While Plee's contention that Fujita ran an experimental program that committed atrocities against Allied prisoners of war is seemingly supported by the language of Fujita's preface, it is not supported by any mention of identifiable individuals or activities related to the war. While the record of the atrocities committed by the trainees at the Futumata Branch of the Nakano School certainly does appear to buttress Plee's conclusion, in that it suggests a pattern of behavior among the most likely organization to have used Fujita's supposed experiments, it is by no means conclusive. The example of the Americans' prosecution of the Futumata Branch cadets is conspicuously absent as it relates to the atrocities Plee claims Fujita committed. It seems all the more difficult to believe that Fujita would have knowingly published a document detailing wartime atrocities, when he would have been well aware of the Allied powers' aggressive post-war prosecution of war crimes.

In the end, while there are intriguing questions and theories surrounding Fujita's role in the Japanese war effort, the seriousness of some of the allegations involved calls for a dispassionate review of the evidence. While Fujita himself claimed that he was involved in the training of the Nakano School cadets, and this claim is widely accepted, there is little else that can be conclusively said about his role, except that it is highly unlikely that Fujita ever led a band of guerillas in Burma. At the end of the war, while hundreds of thousands of Japanese servicemen were still far from their homes—in China, Southeast Asia, and elsewhere—Fujita appears to have been safely in Japan. This is in stark contrast to other Nakano veterans, the prime example of which is Onoda, who languished in the jungles of Lubang for 30 years before returning home to Japan.

An examination of the verifiable evidence of Fujita's activities during the war strongly suggest that he spent most, if not all, of the war in Japan. We know from Fujita's own accounts that he was assigned to the Nakano Spy School from 1937 onward. We also know that he wrote and published *Ninjutsu kara Supai Sen-e* in 1942, which means he would have had to be in Japan to do so, and the publication date coincides exactly with the time he was teaching at Nakano. It could be claimed, however, that the work was composed between 1937 and 1941 and then published in 1942. Fortunately, we have additional sources of evidence from the archives of the Iwata Manzo, which shed additional light on this matter.

Left to right: Iwata, Fujita, Mabuni, at an undisclosed location during the war

It is well known that Fujita was introduced to Iwata by Mabuni Kenwa, founder of Shito-ryu Karate-do, after Iwata enrolled at Toyo University in 1941. Iwata was introduced to Fujita so that he could learn Fujita's Daien-ryu Jojutsu. Recently, there has come to light a menkyo kaiden issued by Fujita in Iwata's name, indicating that Iwata had achieved mastery in Daien-ryu Jojutsu a year after Fujita published *Ninjutsu kara Supai Sen-e*. The fact that the menkyo kaiden was issued in 1943, only two years after Iwata enrolled in Toyo University, strongly suggests that Fujita would have had to be in Japan between 1941 and 1943, since he would not have otherwise been able to train Iwata to menkyo kaiden status in two years.[87] This, coupled with the fact that Fujita was in Japan at the war's end, strongly contradicts the stories that claim Fujita spent much of the war leading a ninja unit in Burma and, instead, suggests that his role was focused on his teaching responsibilities at Nakano.

Thus, in the absence of an identification of the supposed subjects of the experiments mentioned in the preface of *Kempo Gokui Atemi No Sakkatsu-Ho Mekai*, in combination with the identification of the Nihon Bujutsu Kenkyu Jo and the surfacing of the menkyo kaiden issued to Iwata, Plee's entire hypothesis is called into question. This conclusion is supported by both the lack of any attempt on the part of the Allied powers to prosecute Fujita and his obvious lack of concern in publishing the preface in 1958.

The collected evidence demands that we conclude that the allegation is not only unproven but in all probability false. To believe Plee's claim requires that we accept that Fujita had, for 14 years, kept documents that could incriminate him and, then in an even more bizarre twist, decided to publish them. This seems completely incredible and requires corroborating evidence that reconciles the omissions and discrepancies before Plee's theory can be accepted.

FUJITA: RESPECTED MARTIAL ARTIST

With the advent of the ninja boom in the West, there arose unscrupulous characters who attempted to profit from the popularity of ninjutsu by claiming connection to Koga ninjutsu, which was suggested as the logical alternative to the Iga traditions represented by Bujinkan. In some cases, this claim of connection was even more specific, and the name of Fujita was inevitably invoked to assist in making a credible connection that would counter accusations of fraud made by Bujinkan practitioners and others against the supposed Koga ninja. This situation was compounded by the near absence of any factual information related to Fujita in Western languages and gave wide latitude to those interested in benefiting from his career.

This state of affairs led to extreme skepticism and scorn from many circles of the martial arts community toward anything related to Koga ninjutsu, and even mention of Fujita himself raised immediate suspicion, because of his frequent association with dubious claims to a modern Koga ninjutsu tradition. All of this would have come as an extraordinary surprise to Fujita's contemporaries, since his reputation during his lifetime was entirely opposite to the perceptions that developed during the Western ninja boom. The historical record shows that Fujita was a respected martial artist and counted among his friends many of the martial arts luminaries of his day. In the pre-war period, Fujita had associated with numerous Okinawan martial artists. Fujita is recorded as having been both teacher and student to some of the Okinawan masters, with his most notable association being with the illustrious Motobu Choki.

In addition to the Okinawan practitioners who had come to prominence in the 1920s and 1930s, Fujita was also closely associated with numerous koryu artists that were members of the Nihon Kobudo Shinkokai, which was founded in 1935, to preserve traditional Japanese bujutsu (warrior arts). Indeed, Fujita was a fixture at the Nihon Kobudo Shinkokai's annual martial arts demonstration, where he demonstrated various aspects of his prodigious martial arts repertoire.[88] Notable koryu martial artists, who were known associates of Fujita, included Shimizu Takaji, the notable practitioner of Shinto Muso-ryu Jojutsu, an art that was the focus of Fujita's 1953 book, *Shinto Muso-ryu Jojutsu.* Documentation exists to suggest that Shimizu was the source of Fujita's Shinto Muso-ryu knowledge, and Shimizu is listed prominently among those who attended Fujita's funeral.[89] Another martial artist who is usually not thought of as a koryu practitioner is Sakagami Ryusho, a high-level practitioner of kendo and Muso Jikiden-ryu Iaido, who later became a well-known practitioner of Shito-ryu Karate and Taira Shinken's kobojutsu.[90] Another was Nakashima Atsumi, Soke of Katayama Hoki-ryu Jujutsu and Tenjin Myoshin-ryu, as well as a member of Fujita's martial arts research circle. Yet another was Ueno Takahashi, Soke of numerous arts, including Asayama Ichiden-ryu Taijutsu, Bokuden-ryu, Shinto Tenshin-ryu Kempo, Takagi-ryu, Kukishinden-ryu, Shinden Fudo-ryu Taijutsu, Hontai Kijin Chosui-ryu Kukishinden Dakentaijutsu, and Koto-ryu Koppojutsu.[91] Ueno's connection to Fujita is of particular interest to practitioners of modern ninjutsu, since he forms a link between Fujita, who studied various arts with Ueno, and Hatsumi Masaaki, who was for a time in the 1950s Ueno's principal student. It is also notable that Ueno was a student of Takamatsu Toshitsugu, Hatsumi's teacher, and that Ueno received multiple menkyo kaiden from Takamatsu. Fujita himself taught Ueno Nanban Satto-ryu Kempo, which suggests that Ueno had a high regard for Fujita's ability as a martial artist and allows for interesting comparisons between the three most famous men connected to ninjutsu in the modern age.[92]

Indeed, an estimation of Fujita's reputation as a martial artist and scholar is attested to by the famous koryu authority, Donn F. Draeger. In his book, *Comprehensive Asian Fighting Arts*, Draeger states the following about Fujita: "The best sources were the unpublished writings of Fujita Seiko . . ."[93] Even more surprisingly, when compared to the current koryu perspective on ninjutsu, Draeger goes on to make this interesting statement: "The late Fujita Seiko was the last of the living ninja."[94]

Since the advent of the ninja boom in the West, some have argued that Fujita's skills must have been limited, pointing to the fact that Fujita often referred his students to other teachers to acquire certain skills. This could clearly not have been the case, since Fujita was exposed to many famous martial artists, and no negative assessment of his skills exists. Indeed, all of the existing evidence clearly demonstrates that Fujita was held in high esteem by both the practitioners of the Okinawan budo, other gendai (modern) and traditional Japanese koryu. This fact is illustrated by the following quote: "Fujita Seiko (1899-1966)—the 14th head master of the Koga-ryu ninjutsu lineage—he gained the respect of Taira Shinken (1897-1970) and a myriad of other budo authorities including the reverent Ueshiba Morihei (1883-1969), the founder of aikido."[95] An explanation of Fujita's eclectic nature and his willingness to refer his students to others comes down to us in an article in which Fujita describes his martial arts career. His statement is as follows: "I became interested in pursuing the study of budo arts like jujutsu, kendo, shogi, kusarigama, shuriken, jitte, etc. I am currently certified in four arts and have been permitted to study the secrets of four others. Eventually it's possible I will concentrate on kempo. I am Nanban Satto-ryu."[96] The clear inference that can be drawn from this statement is that it was Fujita's prolific curiosity, and not a lack of skill, that drove him to explore the numerous arts available to him.

Another testimonial to Fujita's skills is the fact that he was employed as a bodyguard and investigator by Inoue Saburo, the father of Fujita's famous student, Inoue

Motokatsu. An army general who came from a political family, Inoue Saburo secured Fujita's services at a time when prominent politicians were being assassinated by shadowy Japanese nationalist, connected to the rising fascist tide of the early 1930s.[97] The fact that Inoue Saburo chose Fujita for this task is a strong testimony to his skill, since Inoue, being a prominent man, would surely have had his choice of candidates for the job.

Interestingly, while Fujita remains unheralded among modern ninjutsu practitioners, those connected to the modern Okinawan and Japanese koryu arts are eager to associate their martial arts lineages with him. For example, the modern lineage chart of Ryukyu Kobudo places Fujita among martial arts icons such as Taira, Mabuni, and Funakoshi. The lineage chart mentions him as "Fujita Seiko (Ninja),"[98] a measure of the mystique that his connection to the Koga ninja tradition gave Fujita among his contemporaries and their students. Nowhere is there a more unambiguous testimony to Fujita's notoriety and skill as a martial artist than in a recounting of the list of illustrious martial artists who attended Fujita's funeral when he died in 1966.

"People who attended Fujita's funeral were Shimizu Takaji (Shinto Muso-ryu jojutsu), Sei Kobayashi (Toda-ha Bukou-ryu Naginata ?), Toki Ikeda (Tendou-ryu Naginata ?), Masaru ? Watanabe (Kenyuu/Genyuu-ryu Karate), Akira/Toshi Saitou (Kongan-ryu Shuriken), Kiyonobu? Ogasawara (Ogasawa-ryu Kyuujutsu), Inoue Motokatsu (Okinawa Kobudou Karate), Tani Chojiro (Tani-ha Shito-ryu Karate), Hon Reik? (Muso-ryu Joujutsu), Jjusei Ono (Ono-ha Ittou-ryu). In all cases, these people had highly qualified in martial arts."[99]

SAVING BUJUTSU

In addition to the high esteem in which the martial arts luminaries of the pre-war era held Fujita, it was his post-war activities that would forever ingratiate him to the practitioners of the Japanese martial arts. At the end of the war in August 1945, the Japanese Ministry of Education resumed control of physical education in Japanese public schools, a responsibility that had been handed over to the Dai Nippon Butokukai, the governing body of Japanese martial arts. This venerated organization had itself been hijacked by the Japanese military in 1942, when all martial arts activities were subordinated to the Japanese war effort.

The newly militarized Butokukai also absorbed the Kano Jigoro's Kodokan Judo organization, bringing what was then Japan's most exalted martial art under the yoke of the military. During this period, some of Japan's most prestigious arts were called into question, owing to the Japanese military's perception that they were no longer applicable to modern war. Tournament judo was dismissed as a waste of time, kendo as dancing with bamboo sticks, and kyudo as hopelessly out of date. By the end of the war, the term *budo* applied only to hand-to-hand combat applicable to modern war. In addition to this, classes in arts like jukendo (bayonet) and grenade-tossing became the standard physical education curriculum of Japanese public schools.[100]

This situation brought a backlash against budo from the Supreme Command Allied Powers (SCAP). On October 22, 1945, the SCAP instituted a ban on militaristic and ultra-nationalistic activities, banning even the Butokukai and its military-oriented physical education classes because of the Butokukai's association with the Japanese military government.[101] It was during this period that Fujita established his enduring reputation as one of the saviors of Japan's martial arts. While many post-war Japanese rejected anything remotely associated with the Japanese martial ethos, Fujita fought against what he perceived to be an effort by the SCAP to destroy Japan's already demoralized culture. To this end, although the practice of budo was prohibited, Fujita continued to practice his various arts and to train his students. We now know from his memoirs that Fujita and other martial artists associated with him gathered as much as they could of Japan's historical records related to martial arts in an attempt to ensure their preservation.[102]

On May 28, 1948, almost three years after the ban had been instituted, Japan's martial artists received an invitation to participate in a meeting and a demonstration of the "Ancient Japanese Knight Arts"—an invitation that signaled a softening of the "budo ban." This change in attitude had resulted from many petitions that the SCAP and the Ministry of Education had received from martial artists and the fact that the SCAP had decided that the militaristic spirit had been exorcised from the psyche of the Japanese nation.[103]

In keeping with his character, Fujita took full advantage of this development and chose 1948 as the year in which he openly elevated his two principal students, Inoue and Iwata, to menkyo kaiden status in the various arts that he had passed on to them. The clear inference that any student of the martial arts can draw—an inference supported by Fujita's own activities—is that Fujita had been instructing his students during the time between institution of the "budo ban" and the meeting of the "Ancient Japanese Knights" in 1948.

We also know from the actions of the aforementioned two students that they were ready to spring into action and assist in preserving and spreading Japan's martial traditions. They quickly established training programs that were vital to maintaining these traditions. Iwata's behavior in 1948 entirely supports this conclusion. As soon as he was elevated to menkyo kaiden status by Fujita, Iwata promptly assumed the role of karate coach at the Nihon University Engineering School. In 1950, after the ban was lifted, he founded the Renkukan in Ikenohata and started teaching karate outside Nihon University. In 1951, Iwata became the karate coach at Toyo University, a post that would provide him with an excellent platform to preserve Mabuni's Shito-ryu Karate-do by giving him access to the best young minds that Japan had to offer.[104]

In that same year of 1951, Fujita mirrored Iwata's activities by founding the Nihon Bujutsu Kenkyu Jo, an organization dedicated to the collection and preservation of Japan's traditional martial techniques, collectively known as koryu bujutsu (Ancient Warrior Arts).[105] This organization differed in focus from the efforts of Iwata and Inoue in that it was focused on preserving arts that had been under siege since the modernization of the Meiji era had made Japan's samurai an anachronism. Many practitioners of these arts were forced to abandon their arts in favor of vocations that could earn them a living. In post-Meiji Japan, these arts were no longer of practical utility, and respectable vocations required years of education that would have formerly been dedicated to the practice of the various budo. Thus, many traditional arts died ignominious deaths. This circumstance was further exacerbated by the death of many practitioners during the war, a situation that was compounded by the humiliation of Japan's martial traditions resulting from Japan's the defeat in August 1945.

After the horrific experiences of the war, many ordinary Japanese viewed everything associated with Japan's martial traditions as being related to the folly of the terrible war that had turned their world on its head. In this environment, Fujita and others like him, both from the traditional Japanese arts known as koryu and from the more recently accepted Okinawan arts, were forced to work feverishly to save many of these traditions from oblivion. An example of this can be seen in the training of Fujita's student, Inoue, whom Fujita had initially trained in his own martial arts of Nanban Satto-ryu Kempo, Daien-ryu Jojutsu, and Shingetsu-ryu Shurikenjutsu. Fujita later went on to recommend that Inoue learn various martial skills that fall under the classification of Okinawan kobudo and the Japanese art of Sumo.[106]

It is from this point that Fujita's career as a martial artist, viewed holistically rather than through the lens of the post-war fascination with ninjutsu, and his impact on Japan's martial arts can be understood. While his reputation was inextricably linked to his claim that he was a practitioner of ninjutsu, his peers' estimation of him was more often than not based on skills associated with the samurai traditions and the Okinawan arts of men like Motobu, Mabuni, and Taira. Indeed, during Fujita's lifetime, although he was considered to be the foremost expert in the art of ninjutsu, he adamantly refused to demonstrate any techniques associated with his Wada-ha Koga-ryu, stating that ninjutsu was too dangerous for the modern world and that it had become an anachronism. What Fujita did demonstrate as being related to ninjutsu were feats that he claimed were intended to show the dedication and commitment inculcated by ninjutsu training. Others, however, have claimed that these demonstrations were more in keeping with the skills he learned from the Yamabushi, since they most often involved demonstrating high levels of pain tolerance.

In combination with Fujita's training in both Japanese and Okinawan martial artists, his prolific writings on numerous subjects related to the martial arts preserved and disseminated aspects of the Japanese martial arts that might otherwise have been lost in Japan's post-war ambivalence toward all things traditional. Indeed, Fujita's preservation efforts were considered so important that, as previously mentioned, he was not only a fixture at the annual demonstration of the Nihon Kobudo Shinkokai, but he was also a member of the board of trustees of the venerable organization, an honor that was due in no small part to his reputation as a martial arts scholar and historian. Fujita's friend and fellow martial artist Kunii Zen'ya, 18th generation Shihan-ke of Kashima Shin-ryu, summarized the importance of Fujita's research and preservation efforts at his funeral: "Because he was also famous for researching ancient writings we deplore his death more than we could say, however, we believe in the immortality of his soul."[107]

PASSING ON THE SYSTEMS

In the 40 years since Fujita's death, much has been made over the fate of his martial knowledge, most particularly the fate of his Wada-ha Koga-ryu Ninjutsu, the area most often focused on because of the ninja boom in Japan and the West. The true fate of Fujita's martial arts, however, can be understood only when examined from the point of view of his total martial arts repertoire, particularly as it concerns the three other arts for which he held the position of Soke, namely, Nanban Satto-ryu Kempo, Daien-ryu Jojutsu, and Shingetsu-ryu Shurikenjutsu.[108]

An evaluation of Fujita's martial legacy must involve balancing our modern understanding of his martial arts, which again is colored by the mystery surrounding his Wada-ha Koga-ryu Ninjutsu, juxtaposed with the official history of Fujita's career, as recorded in his own words, and in the words of those who knew him. As I established in the previous chapter, Fujita was interested in and worked to preserve Japan's martial traditions when they were threatened with extinction.

We know that Fujita not only worked to add to his martial knowledge through apprenticeships with other martial artists such as Motobu, Taira and Ueno, but we also know that Fujita passed on his knowledge to other martial artists, particularly Inoue Motokatsu and Iwata Manzo. It is in the experiences of these two students that we have the clearest picture of the facts as to the fate of Fujita's martial knowledge.

Inoue Motokatsu

Inoue Motokatsu was born in 1918 to a noble family. He was the son of an army general, Inoue Saburo, and the great grandson (on his mother's side) of Inoue Kaoru, a Koshaku (Prince) and former prime minister of Japan. His grandfather, Inoue Katsunosuke, was ambassador to Britain from 1913 to 1917. Inoue's privileged position afforded him access to opportunities not commonly available to others, and he began the customary training in the bujutsu traditions early. Inoue's first teacher was Fujita, who served as his father's bodyguard, and to whom Inoue was entrusted at age 10 to learn jujutsu. Inoue considered Fujita to be "a very mysterious martial artist" and "a true master, capable of many strange feats including the ability to disregard pain."[109]

Inoue further observed Fujita's style of martial arts, contrasting it with the popular martial arts of karate and aikido. According to Inoue, Fujita thought that karate was "too linear" and that aikido was "too circular."[110] Inoue described Fujita's style as "a very aggressive form of jujutsu and aiki, with particular emphasis on attacking the eyes, throat and groin, using open hand techniques and low kicks." He further mentioned that "Fujita was also a skilled master of numerous weapons, with a 'preference to those peculiar to ninjutsu.'"[111] Fujita taught the young Inoue to become adept at throwing any object that was available, with an emphasis on training with shuriken. These projectile-throwing techniques were the central focus of Fujita's Shingetsu-ryu Shurikenjutsu, a traditional samurai system. The Shingetsu-ryu included an array of different types of shuriken, including knife and short arrow-like projectiles, as well as the more commonly known star-shaped shaken. Fujita also taught Inoue Daien-ryu Jojutsu, an art that used a staff measuring about 50 inches in length and about one inch in diameter.[112] Daien-ryu is the same staff art that Fujita favored in his younger days when he often got into street fights.

By the time he was 18 years old, Inoue had a good understanding of jujutsu, shurikenjutsu, and jojutsu. Fujita encouraged Inoue to become adept in a wide range of martial arts and even ordered him to join the Sumo club of Keio University, once he was enrolled as a student. Fujita was convinced that Inoue would benefit from the taisabaki (body movement) of Sumo, and consequently, Inoue had acquired a thorough grounding in Sumo by the time he graduated.

In addition to Sumo, Fujita instructed Inoue to study karate with Konishi Yasuhiro, his notable colleague and sometime student. Fujita selected Konishi as Inoue's karate instructor because Konishi practiced a "jutsu" form that was oriented to combat, rather than a "do" form that focused on spiritual development. When Inoue had completed his training in karate, Fujita sent him to Shioda Gozo, one of aikido founder Ueshiba Morihei's top disciples and a practitioner of a more combat-oriented version of aikido, Yoshin Aikido. Shioda moved Inoue up to third Dan before Inoue had completed his training.

The last teacher that Fujita selected for Inoue was the well-known Okinawan practitioner, Taira Shinken. Taira was considered by many to be the greatest Okinawan kobudo master of his day. Inoue developed a close relationship with Taira and decades later, would become his most important student and inheritor.[113] Fujita himself participated in Inoue's training with Taira, as did his friend Sakagami Ryusho, who also undertook extensive training with Taira.[114]

While there is clear evidence that Inoue did learn a great deal from Fujita, Inoue neither claimed to have learned the secrets of Wada-ha Koga-ryu, nor is there any evidence to suggest that Fujita passed on these secrets to his young apprentice. Indeed, Fujita's approach to training Inoue appears to have been eclectic, and he seems to have encouraged Inoue and others to study a wide range of martial arts, not only because of an experimental bent that was common among Japanese martial artists of Fujita's day but also to ensure that the ancient skills would be preserved.

Fujita, Taira, Sakagami, Inoue

When Fujita finally gave Inoue permission to open a dojo in Shimizu city in 1948, it was so that Inoue could teach Yuishinkai Karate-jutsu, a composite style that Fujita had named and co-founded and that retained qualities of traditional bujutsu, such as jujutsu and shurikenjutsu. Inoue also taught the traditional Okinawan Ryukyu kobojutsu that he had learned from Konishi and Taira.

Inoue's art is described as being similar to Wado Ryu, another composite style, and is characterized by stances and softness in blocking that testify to the influence of jujutsu in its formation. Once the basics (which include ten sets of break falls, punches, and knee and elbow attacks) are mastered, Inoue then taught kata of the Shito style. Inoue does not mention ninjutsu as being among the techniques that were taught to him. Indeed, while he does mention jujutsu, Daien-ryu Jojutsu, and Shingetsu-ryu Shurikenjutsu, for which he received the rank of Shihan shortly before Fujita's death, Inoue's only mention of ninjutsu was to credit his mentor, Fujita, as being the 14th Soke of the Wada-ha Koga-ryu.[115]

A testimony by those closest to Fujita, such as his family and martial arts colleagues, does exist to give us an idea of their perceptions of Fujita's relationship with his students and peers. Fujita's obituary mentions Inoue as being present at his mentor's funeral. Inoue does not, however, assume the place traditionally reserved for an inheritor of his teacher's mantle. Indeed, while Fujita clearly played a considerable role in Inoue's development, his obituary testifies to the fact that he saw his young pupil as a master of arts, but of arts other than those with which Fujita was most closely associated. Inoue is described in this way: "Inoue Motokatsu, Okinawan Kobudo Karate."[116]

To find the person who was the most likely to have inherited Fujita's position as head of the Wada-ha Koga-ryu, assuming that the system was passed on to someone, we must look at his other famous student, Iwata Manzo. It was Iwata who assumed the customary role reserved for one who inherits his master's knowledge, and indeed, Fujita's obituary mentions Iwata as his uchi-deshi.[117]

Iwata Manzo

Iwata Manzo's karate teacher, Mabuni Kenwa, founder of Shito-ryu Karate-do referred Iwata to Fujita. Mabuni was known as an open-minded and talented martial artist who was interested in the research and preservation of Japanese martial arts. Mabuni ran a martial arts study group from his home that was attended by many of Okinawa's martial arts luminaries, including Chibana Chosin, Funakoshi Gichin, Shiroma Shinpan, Tokuda Anbun, Oshiro Choju, Tokumura Seicho, and Ishikawa Hoko. Mabuni was well aware of each system's deficiencies and decided to include the traditional bujutsu techniques of gyaku waza and nage waza in his Shito-ryu Karate-do. These techniques are mentioned in Shito-ryu Karate-do, in association with Mabuni's friend, Fujita.[118] The inclusion of these techniques in his system stands as testimony to Mabuni's respect for Fujita's martial abilities. This fact was further demonstrated when Mabuni decided that his top student, Iwata, was suited to study jojutsu and thus recommended that Iwata study with Fujita.

Fujita and Iwata practicing jojutsu

Iwata was born on February 9, 1924. At the age of 10, he was introduced to Shito-ryu Karate-do, and like many young men of his day, he also learned judo and kendo. He was also exposed to aikido by a friend of his father, Ueshiba Morihei, the art's founder. Around the time he was 18 years old, Iwata began to train with Mabuni directly, when he enrolled at Toyo University in 1941. Iwata's meeting with Mabuni was a fateful one, which not only set Iwata along the path that would lead to him to become a well-known proponent of karate but also led to him being apprenticed to Fujita.

Iwata trained with Fujita in the art of jojutsu for two years, and in 1943, Iwata was ranked by Fujita as a Shihan (master) of Daien-ryu Jojutsu. Over the next few years, Iwata continued to train with Fujita as his uchi-deshi. In 1948, Iwata was endowed by Fujita with the title of Soke, commanding him to assume all of the hereditary knowledge of Fujita's Nanban Satto-ryu Kempo, Shingetsu-ryu Shurikenjutsu, and Daien-ryu Jojutsu.[119]

Iwata later went on to a storied career as Hanshi (senior master) of Shito-ryu Karate-do and would, upon reflection, pay his respects to Fujita by saying, "All I obtained from master Fujita was a valuable asset and I am particularly grateful for master Mabuni's recommendation"—a considerable accolade from a man who had studied with the martial arts icons such as Ueshiba and Mabuni.[120]

Fujita's evident confidence in Iwata, as demonstrated by Iwata's inheritance of three of Fujita's systems, provides an interesting window into the way Fujita viewed his 4th system, Wada-ha Koga-ryu. Again, having confirmed Iwata's inheritance of Fujita's arts, what then was so different about Fujita's Wada-ha Koga-ryu that Fujita refrained from passing it on to one of his prominent students?

We know from Fujita's obituary that Iwata was selected for the place of honor customarily reserved for an uchi-deshi. Iwata is documented to be the inheritor of Fujita's Nanban Satto-ryu Kempo, Daien-ryu Jojutsu, and Shingetsu-ryu Shurikenjutsu. But the same obituary states that Fujita, a man who had worked all his life to collect and preserve the martial knowledge of Japan, had chosen not to train an inheritor for his Wada-ha Koga-ryu and was, therefore, the "last ninja." What appears clear from all of the evidence is that had Fujita named an inheritor to his Wada-ha Koga-ryu, it would surely have been Iwata.

The lack of evidence suggesting that Fujita passed on his Wada-ha Koga-ryu, especially when contrasted with the clear record of Fujita's conferring of his other systems upon Iwata, strongly suggests that Fujita did not pass on his Wada-Ha Koga-ryu. However, the absence of definitive evidence one way or the other is unsatisfactory in the face of conflicting claims to Fujita's legacy. This is all the more the case when we consider that more than one of the many claimants to Fujita's Wada-ha Koga-ryu have suggested that Fujita reverted to the pre-modern outlook on ninjutsu and passed on Wada-ha Koga-ryu clandestinely.

Iwata Manzo in his family samurai armor

Fortunately for martial artists and researchers, this unsatisfactory state of affairs is addressed by Fujita himself and is recorded in the historical record. These records address the apparent ambiguity as to the fate of the Wada-ha Koga-ryu. These historical records specifically deal with the questions of why Fujita passed on all of his martial arts systems to the likes of Inoue and Iwata, with the exception of Wada-ha Koga-ryu—the system that was the pillar of his reputation as a martial artist.

THE LAST KOGA NINJA

In 1958, Fujita wrote a book, which he titled *Doron Doron: Saigo No Ninja* (The Last Ninja), recounting how his grandfather passed on the secrets of his family Wada-ha Koga-ryu system to him. The book, which was published 10 years after Fujita elevated Iwata to the position of Soke of Nanban Satto-ryu Kempo and Shingetsu-ryu Shurikenjutsu, implies that even at this late date, he had not passed his Wada-ha Koga-ryu system on to any of his students or associates.

Additional support for this conclusion is also available in an interview Fujita conducted with the official authority on the history of Japanese martial traditions, the *Bugei Ryuha Daijiten*, which at the time was gathering information from the heads of various traditional Japanese martial arts systems for its updated publication. The interview appeared in the 1963 edition and was later reprinted in the 1978 annotated and revised edition, written by Watatani Kiyoshi and Yamada Tadashi. The interview with Fujita took place in his capacity as the Soke of Wada-ha Koga-ryu. The entry on Fujita's information for the Wada-ha Koga-ryu is as follows: "This ryu is one of the 53 Koga families. Moreover, this ryuha is one of the Minami-yama Rokke of only 6 families, and nobody knows this ryuha." Watatani then attributes the quote to "Fujita Seiko, 1963."[121]

In the 1978 revision, Watatani then summarized and reflected on Fujita's information: "So here Fujita Seiko was the last Soke of this ryuha and it was one of 6 ryu that belonged to the Minami-yama Rokke, maybe 6 strong families or an organization." He ends his reflection in a very telling way when he writes, "Also, nobody knows this ryuha today. I think he never taught it."[122] This is a powerful verdict from a man who is the author of Japan's official "Martial Arts Directory."[123] This statement by Watatani, absent valid evidence contradicting it, must be considered martial arts canon.

Two additional entries in the 1978 edition mention Fujita, one that is simply entered as "Wada Ryu," and which is said to be the same as Wada-ha Koga-ryu. The entry mentions that a "Wada Iga-No-Kami Koremasa founded the ryu, [and that] Fujita Seiko is a descendent of his."[124] The entry provides a very compelling piece of evidence that the Wada-ha Koga-ryu was transmitted through Fujita's family and coincides with the evidence that he genuinely believed he was Soke of the last Koga ninja tradition. In another entry, Fujita makes an "educated guess" about another school, saying it was known as "Wada To."[125] Watatani then states that in his opinion this was only a guess, which is testimony to the fact that Fujita's expertise extended only to Wada-ha Koga-ryu, a fact starkly at odds with those fraudulent claimants in the West who make generic claims that Fujita was Soke of a general system called 'Koga-ryu.'

The most interesting information that emerges from Watatani's interview, however, is Fujita's clear insistence that he had not taught the system to anyone, and Watatani's subsequent conclusion that Fujita was the last Soke of Wada-ha Koga-ryu. The impact of such a statement, given the authority of Watatani's publication, is clear. The entry of the statement into the record, whether factual or not, would relegate all future claimants to a linear inheritance of the system to the ranks of charlatans and con-artists.

Only one conclusion is supported by both Fujita's own accounts and independent documentary evidence. Fujita, a man who had spent his entire life practicing and trying to preserve the traditional martial arts of Japan, had, just three short years before his death, unalterably decided he would be, as his 1958 book declared, "The Last (Koga) Ninja." The question, then, is: why was he so intent on a course of action that seemed so at odds with his life's work? What was it about this Wada-ha Koga-ryu that made it so different from his other martial arts systems of Daien-ryu Jojutsu, Nanban Satto-ryu Kempo and Shingetsu-ryu Shurikenjutsu? The answer appears to lie in the unique nature of ninjutsu. The evidence to support this conclusion has emerged from records of another interview that took place two years before Fujita died.

PRESERVING THE ART'S INTEGRITY

To understand the reasons why Fujita decided to consign his hereditary family ninjutsu system to the list of extinct Japanese martial arts from the pre-modern period requires reflection on the nature of ninjutsu in Japanese history. Unlike the samurai arts that had evolved with Japan through the long peace of the Tokugawa Shogunate, and further still after the Meiji modernization, ninjutsu had always been an underground and illegal subculture that remained beyond the scope of government decrees. The martial arts historian Donn F. Draeger reminds us that ninjutsu had developed among an oppressed class of people that depended on secrecy for survival. He writes: "Below the rank of the commoner were the so-called hinin 'nonhumans.' . . ."[126] Draeger then goes on to mention that the ninja often came from this shunned class, the hinin, and thus, ninjutsu had always thrived for the very reason that it was a close-knit system that was completely hidden from anyone outside its immediate family circle.

It had been historical practice, at least since the long peace of the Tokugawa Shogunate, for the last inheritor of a ninjutsu system to destroy all of the records and secrets of the system if no worthy inheritor was found. Indeed, Fujita himself mentions that being born into a family that practiced ninjutsu did not guarantee that a child would be trained in ninjutsu. No less a figure than Morinosuke, Fujita's father, demonstrated this—for while he was clearly a talented martial artist and a respected policeman, Shintazaemon decided not to pass ninjutsu onto him and only trained Fujita after he demonstrated an extraordinary ability to endure hardship, as evidenced by his experiences with the Yamabushi. This practice had become the common resort of ninjutsu inheritors, since the stability of the new era relegated their arcane skills to irrelevance and compelled ninjutsu practitioners to pursue peacetime vocations to support their families. This practice eventually led to the near extinction of the art, which, before the openness of the 20th century, was considered to be a fact. Additionally, it had always been acceptable to destroy a system to prevent its falling into disrepute. Fujita himself wrote the following about just such a matter: "In order to ensure the future prosperity for each family, there were protocols. Those who revealed the secrets of their systems would without a doubt be assassinated."[127] Evidence suggests that this is exactly the way Fujita perceived the situation as it existed at the time that he was training both Inoue and Iwata.

In post-World War II Japan, such a set of circumstances existed. The old rules no longer applied, and the old schools of the samurai, which had evolved into classical and then modern budo, were being taught to the American occupiers, whom Fujita had fought during the war and who, he believed, had banned the martial arts as a means of destroying Japanese culture. Fujita was further troubled by the fact that other Japanese martial artists, such as Hatsumi Yoshiaki (who later changed his name to Masaaki), and Hatsumi's teacher, Takamatsu, were opening the sacred teachings of ninjutsu to public scrutiny. The most glaring examples of this public exposure were stories that appeared in the *Tokyo Times*, on Monday, March 6, 1966, related to Hatsumi's role as advisor to the producers of the James Bond movie "You Only Live Twice,"[128] and the 1967 release of *Black Belt Magazine's* second and third issues to the western martial arts community. The two releases contained articles featuring Hatsumi demonstrating various ninjutsu techniques—a clear departure from the days when even speaking the art's name was taboo.[129]

In Japan, 'ninja mania' was far more advanced. As early as October 1957, the English martial artist Richard Bowen had written an article for the publication *Budokwai Quarterly Judo*, which catalogued various misdeeds committed by individuals who were taking interpretation of ninjutsu beyond the bounds of legality.[130] A measure of Fujita's displeasure with this state of affairs is evident in an interview he gave just two years before he died. In this interview with a journalist for the Tokyo-based *Sankei Shimbun*, Fujita, then 65 years old, recounted his training with his grandfather and the various rigors of his regimen: "I ate sulfuric acid, rat poison, lizards, 879 glasses and 30 bricks." The article then goes on to say that "Fujita claims he is the last ninja and the secrets of the art will die with [him]. The article then reveals the central reason for this decision: that Fujita "deplores the current commercialization of the ninja in Japan."[131] While we take it for granted today, the public exposure and commercialization of the art were indeed a dramatic departure from the traditions of the art.

The exposure of the art to persons other than members of the immediate clan or family was strictly proscribed and was akin to committing religious sacrilege in European medieval times. Here, then, is the most probable reason why Fujita, who had worked all his life to perfect his skills and preserve the arts of his ancestors, decided to relegate the Wada-ha Koga-ryu to extinction. To not do so was a far greater affront to his family tradition than allowing it to die.

Fujita, it seems, was a man living outside of his time. He was unable to reconcile himself to the fact that the world had changed so utterly and that his treasured ninjutsu was openly being manipulated for commercial and entertainment purposes. Thus, the evidence suggests, Fujita decided to overlook his students and martial arts colleagues as potential inheritors of the Wada-ha Koga-ryu and instead decided to consign this last remaining system of Koga ninjutsu system to history.

Fujita's behavior in relation to his Wada-ha Koga-ryu, while difficult to understand from the perspective of a world in which ninjutsu is no longer a carefully guarded and mysterious secret, was nonetheless the historical norm. Hatsumi's openness, which has led to the preservation of the art in the guise of the Bujinkan, is the traditional exception.

In Fujita's obituary, we have the last testimony connected to him, and it contains an unambiguous statement as to the fate of Fujita's Wada-ha Koga-ryu tradition. Once again, as with the title of his biography, the title of his obituary is telling: *The Last Ninja Disappears.* In addition to the clear inference that can be drawn from this title, there are other clear statements that Fujita, his family, his students, and his peers saw him as the last practitioner of an arcane art.

The Last Ninja Disappears, Fujita's obituary as published in Nikan Kanko

Fujita's friend, Sakagami Ryusho, states the following: "He (Fujita) was the last one who was fully perservering in his training, with him ends all Koga-ryu Ninpo and ninjutsu." Iwata, declared the inheritor of Fujita's knowledge in the obituary, is listed as being the 4th Soke of Nanban Satto-ryu Kempo. No mention is made of inheriting or being trained in the mysterious art of Wada-ha Koga-ryu, and a reason why this might have been the case is given. Fujita is quoted as stating that attaining the skills of the ninja required a diligence that was not possible in our comfortable modern life because of the commitment and dangers involved. The most poignant statement concerning the fate of the Wada-ha Koga Ryu harkens back to the day in 1910 when Fujita assumed the mantle of Soke, with words that Shintazaemon spoke to him: "The orthodox Koga-ryu will be ended after you." Shintazaemon's words are uncompromising, and Fujita may have heard in them the force of a command, thereby leaving him with no choice.[132]

The martial arts writer and researcher Andrew Adams, who published his famous book *Ninja: The Invisible Assassins*, in 1970, helps to validate the fact that Wada-ha Koga-ryu was considered to have died with Fujita. Adams states that at the time, "Hatsumi has been honored by being the only ninja listed in Japan's official Martial Arts Directory."[133] This statement was made ten years before the American ninja boom and a mere four years after Fujita's death, and therefore, it cannot be dismissed as a Bujinkan ploy to benefit from being the sole source of the art. This charge would be put forward a decade later when the Western ninjutsu pioneer Stephen K. Hayes made the same statement in 1980. Indeed, this statement by Adams, who was not a practitioner of ninjutsu but an impartial researcher, allows for an unbiased reflection on the facts as they existed in 1970.

As usual with Fujita, his actions are as strong and compelling as his words, for shortly before his death, he donated his ninjutsu-related belongings to the Ninja Museum at Iga-Ueno, a fact that is attested to by Stephen Turnbull. Turnbull also mentions the Ninja Museum, saying that "among other things it has the archive of books, clothing and weapons belonging to the 'last ninja' Fujita Seiko."[134]

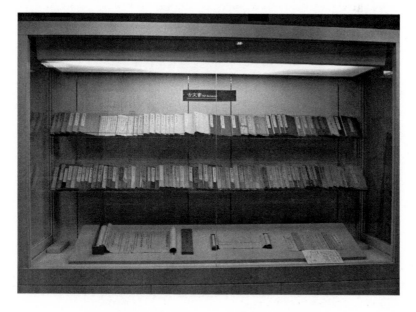

The Fujita Bunko (Library) in Iga-Ueno Museum

The belief that all of Fujita's ninjutsu-related materials were willed to the Iga-Ueno museum persisted until recently, when in the course of doing research for this project, I discovered that some ninjutsu-related documents that can be clearly connected to Fujita are actually in the Iwata family archive. It appears that Fujita had passed various documents on to Iwata, perhaps as early as 1948, when Fujita elevated Iwata to the position of Soke of Nanban Satto-ryu Kempo. These items, which can be indisputably connected to Fujita, were photographed by Jose Luis Calderoni, a student of Murayama, Iwata's uchi-deshi. Calderoni photographed certain items in the Iwata family archive while undertaking karate instruction at the Iwata family residence. The photographs were taken in the Iwata family's living room, with the express permission of Iwata, and were donated to this project by Calderoni's friend and fellow student of Murayama, Sam Moledzki, in whose care the photos have been for several years.[135]

These documents include, among other things, an interesting ukiyo-e (floating world) screen print that appears at the beginning of Fujita's book, *Ninjutsu Hiroku* (Ninjutsu In-Depth), which was published in 1936.[136] An examination of various photographs of this screen print clearly shows that the screen print is the same item that appears in Fujita's book, down to the particular creasing caused by the folding of the print. The possibility that the photographs of the printing might have been duplicated from the book is eliminated by the fact that the photographs are in color and are highly detailed. In contrast, the original in Fujita's book is a black-and-white print that is relatively unclear. Additional items related to ninjutsu in the Iwata family archive are photographs of two sets of densho, the *Iga-Koga Ninjutsu Hikan Bansenshukai*, which are laid out in traditional format and include a single photograph of the contents of these densho showing shuriken and other ninjutsu-related equipment.

Photo of the Bansenshukai in the Iwata collection

While the surfacing of documents in the Iwata family archive that can be clearly connected to Fujita deviates from previously accepted history, it must be clearly understood that the Iwata family does not claim to have inherited Fujita's Wada-ha Koga-ryu. Indeed, the story of Fujita's career, as conveyed by the practitioners of the Shito-Kai, which is the branch of Shito-ryu most closely associated with the Iwata family, clearly states that Fujita was the last practitioner of the Wada-ha Koga-ryu.[137]

Iwata, it is clear, was Fujita's primary disciple, and this new evidence reinforces the fact that had Fujita selected an inheritor for his ninjutsu system, it would have certainly been Iwata. This fact is openly and proudly proclaimed by Iwata Genzo, who, since Iwata Manzo's death in 1993, has been Soke of Nanban Satto-ryu Kempo, Shingetsu-ryu Shurikenjutsu, and Daien-ryu Jojutsu. As is the tradition among Japanese martial artists, the primary student claims to have been the only student, and to that end, Iwata Genzo said the following: "He [Fujita] wrote many books, but his knowledge was transmitted only to master Iwata Manzo."[138] The facts are clear. All the evidence from Fujita himself, the Iwata family, and all those who knew Fujita declare that he left no successor to the Wada-ha Koga-ryu, a fact that was put beyond doubt when Fujita bequeathed the vast majority of his ninjutsu materials to the Iga-Ueno museum.

This last action on the part of Fujita is completely antithetical to the idea that he designated an inheritor to his Wada-ha Koga-ryu. This would have been an unprecedented act in Japanese martial tradition. The inheritor of a system would invariably receive any such items, as a way to demonstrate an unbroken line of transmission from one generation to the next. This, as much as any of Fujita's words, signifies his breaking of the master-student connection that has always been the medium of transmission of traditional Japanese martial knowledge. It stands as tangible evidence to accompany Fujita's spoken intentions. In the absence of clear documentary evidence of transmission from Fujita to one of his students, the combination of his words and actions is unquestionable. Anyone claiming inheritance of the Wada-ha Koga-ryu, in the absence of verifiable documentation, must reconcile themselves to the fact that their connection to the Wada-ha Koga-ryu is, in the best light, purely inspirational and certainly not factual.

In the end, it seems that Fujita was, as he intended, the "last ninja" of the Wada-ha Koga-ryu. All of Fujita's behavior, from his selection of the title *Doron Doron: Saigo No Ninja* (The Last Ninja), to his interviews with Watatani in 1963 and the *Sankei Shimbun* in 1964, paints a picture of a man who saw ninjutsu through traditional eyes. The evidence can only be interpreted to mean that this had been Fujita's long-held intention. Finally, Fujita's intentions are beyond doubt when we recall his own words to the *Sankei Shimbun*. In reference to the Wada-ha Koga-ryu, Fujita said that the art "will die with me." When Fujita died of cirrhosis of the liver on January 4, 1966, at his home in Tokyo, the title of his 1958 book became prophetic.[139]

FUJITA'S LEGACY[140]

For Fujita, an examination of the facts of his career reconfirms his reputation as a mysterious martial artist. Today, and in his own day, Fujita was primarily known for his connection to ninjutsu, a system that he decided had outlived its purpose.[141] Today, however, his reputation is mysteriously intact among a branch of styles that emanated from traditional Okinawan kobudo. The same is also true of Fujita's reputation among the koryu arts and is evidenced by the fact that his successor, Iwata Manzo, and his son, Iwata Genzo, conducted demonstrations of Fujita's Nanban Satto-ryu Kempo for the Nihon Kobudo Shinkokai at its annual Taikai, in both 1990 and 1995.[142]

Another important aspect of Fujita's legacy can be seen in his attempts to preserve Japan's martial traditions in the form of books and articles related to the traditional arts of Japan and Okinawa. This fact is particularly poignant when we consider the environment in Japan at the end of the war and the probability that many of these arts would have become extinct had it not been for efforts of men like Fujita. Fujita's importance in preserving and spreading the martial arts is further attested to not only by his founding of the Ninhon Bujutsu Kenkyo Jo and the fact that he was a trustee of the Nihon Kobudo Shinkokai but also by the role that his students Iwata and Inoue have had in spreading budo.

Fujita, who is known primarily for his study of traditional bujutsu and not the Okinawan arts, nonetheless made an enduring impression on the masters of these traditions. Students of men such as Mabuni, Taira, and Konishi relate to us the strange story of the contributions Fujita made to the modern Okinawan-based martial systems. From Fujita's association with the bujutsu techniques of gyaku waza and nage waza in the Shito-ryu Karate-do, to his co-founding of Yuishinkai Karate-jutsu with Inoue, his eclectic legacy is exemplified by his appearance on the lineage chart of Ryukyu-Kobudo.com, the website of that system's Honbu dojo. However, it is in the Shito-Kai branch of Shito-ryu that Fujita's influence was most profound. The replacement of the Shito-ryu's Bunkai Kumite with techniques taken from Nanban Satto-ryu Kempo, as was taught by Iwata to his son Iwata Genzo, exemplifies the radical and transformative effect that Fujita had on those who came under his influence.

Paradoxically, Fujita comes down to us as a man with two diametrically opposed reputations: he had worked all his life to preserve the traditional martial arts of Japan while at the same time influencing them to combine into eclectic forms that are illustrated by the martial arts of his student Inoue. In relation to his impact on ninjutsu, Fujita is again a complex combination of divergent forces. He stated in his interview with the *Sankei Shimbun* that he deplored the commercialization of the art associated with Japan's ninja boom; however, he played a fundamental part in the popularization of the art both before and after the war, as evidenced by his publication of half a dozen books on the subject. Indeed, during the height of the ninja boom, around the time of the 1964 Tokyo Olympics, Fujita attempted to convince the Japanese Olympic Committee to adopt ninjutsu leaping techniques to afford Japanese athletes an advantage.[143]

Despite his many contradictions, what can be said of Fujita is that he clearly had a profound impact on the martial arts of Japan during the 20th century. It is true that Fujita could not divorce himself from his pre-war vision of Japan, which drove him to act for reasons other than those most modern Japanese would advocate. In doing so, however, Fujita and others like him helped to preserve, first for Japan and later for the world, the ancient arts that many of us practice today.

In light of the scope of his work related to the martial arts—whether in the form of learning numerous arts, participating in numerous research and preservation societies, or writing various books—Fujita cannot be dismissed as a mere vehicle used by frauds to substantiate their dubious claims. The evidence strongly suggests that the conventional wisdom, as seen in light of the ninja boom, does not tell us the whole story. While it is certain from his own words that the Wada-ha Koga-ryu system died with him, what is now equally certain is that there is another intriguing aspect to this complicated man. Fujita's mention in the *Bugei Ryuha Daijiten*, the high regard his contemporaries afforded him, and the acknowledged contributions Fujita made to their arts demand an intellectually impartial revisiting of his influence on the modern martial arts. In the final analysis, it appears clear that when the last chapter of his story comes to light and our time's momentary fascination with ninjutsu has passed, Fujita Seiko's legacy will turn out to be far more than is suggested by his own self-proclaimed title, the "last ninja."

EPILOGUE

As I wrote this biography of Fujita Seiko, several interesting problems came to light. The first was the task of sifting through a cornucopia of rumor and myth to arrive at some strand of supported fact. This problem was further compounded by having to pry the smallest bit of information from individuals who were reticent to cooperate, either out of fear that they might assist yet another person attempting to use Fujita's name for fraudulent purposes, or who guarded even the faintest sliver of fact as though it were some sort of sacred esoterica.

Another interesting challenge involved adjusting my mind-set away from the preconception that information would exist in a ninjutsu context, to a more flexible approach that mirrored the mentality of the Fujita himself. This approach would ultimately yield the most productive information.

The last hurdle to compiling this information was the personality of Fujita himself. All of the extant information about the first three decades of his life was documented by Fujita himself and portrays his exploits in the fantastic, and indeed near mythic, dimensions. This type of depiction is common both to traditional martial arts lore and to someone with a predilection for self-aggrandizement. It must be said, however, that both Fujita's students and the photographic information available suggest that any exaggeration is not without substantial basis in fact.

There are numerous individuals who made the completion of this work possible. First and foremost, I would like to thank Sam Moledzki, Shihan, a senior practitioner of Shito-ryu Karate, whose connection to the Iwata family, via his teacher Murayama Kunio, Shihan, made it possible for him to contribute invaluable documentary and photographic information to this project. I would also like to thank Murayama Sensei for graciously allowing me to interview him about the details of his apprenticeship under Iwata Manzo and for honoring me by allowing me to be his uke at several Satto-ryu Kempo seminars. These seminars allowed me an unparalleled window into the substance of what Fujita Seiko had to teach. The following individuals were instrumental in making possible the translation of Fujita Seiko's works. First, Makoto Tomizuka, a Japanese language professional, worked on Fujita's autobiography and obituary for this project. Second, I thank Nathan Scott for translating Nihon Kobudo Shinkokai documents related to Nanban Satto-ryu Kempo. In addition I would also like to acknowledge Robert C. Gruzanski for contributing information from the collection of his acclaimed father, Charles V. Gruzanski. I would also like to mention Andrew K. Jones, for contributing various articles from his collection, and Eric Weil, for transcribing information from the Bugei Ryuha Daijiten. Also I thank George Kolher, for his willingness to liberally impart his considerable knowledge to anyone interested in budo. There are several other individuals whom I would like to acknowledge for reviewing my work and making suggestions that were indispensable to me. To my wife, Christy, my brother-in-law, Luis Garcia, and my friend Brian Jang, thank you.

In embarking upon this project, I wanted to address a gaping hole in the story of budo in general and ninjutsu in particular. I had hoped to present a particular truth to counter the mosaic of lies that so often accompanies the mention of Fujita's name. Instead, I find that I have arrived at the Fujita mythos, as seen through his words and in those of his students. I am sure that this work will have its critics. Some will say that I have given potential frauds too much information. Others, that I have been too uncritical of Fujita's eccentricities and claims. Others still will find mistakes in the work or facts that I did not uncover. All of this I welcome, on the path to further understanding of this mysterious man.

APPENDIX

LETTER OF IWATA GENZO TO SAM MOLEDZKI

Mr. Sam Moledzki:

Thank you very much for your kind attentions during our stay at the Pan-American Championship held in Puebla. After this, how have you been?

You have asked me the story about my father. Unfortunately I have not had enough time to do it until now. I have found a magazine called Karate-Do, which contains a special report about Shito-ryu and my father Manzo Iwata.

I send you a copy of such magazine, there you will find all what you need. Select what you consider necessary. Congratulations, and hope this letter finds you well in company of your family.

Iwata Genzo.

In the history of Karate there has been several famous men: some became masters and others great fighters. Some of them were bound by friendship, others remained distant, but all of them maintained the philosophy, techniques, spirit and discipline that has continued today.

A young man in the noble discipline of Shito-ryu Karate, the path to follow along with his fellow students and his Master. Some youngsters are born in this way and continue with the tradition and school that his father taught him.

Soke, is a form the Japanese culture for the son that will continue the tradition, generation through generation. This magazine the story of the founder of Karate-Do Shito-ryu, of his teachings, his spirit, his style, together with several pictures.

Number 2

The founder of Shito-ryu, martial artist from Okinawa, Kenwa Mabuni. Manzo Iwata, student of Master Mabuni, spread Karate throughout the western part of Japan and kept friendly links with many Karateka and martial artist from other styles, and descendant No. 14 of founder of Koga-ryu ninja, Master Seiko Fujita, which granted Manzo Iwata Nanban Satoryu Kempo, Daien Ryu Jodo and Shingetsu Ryu Shuriken.

Number 3
By Master Kenwa Mabuni.

Kenei Mabuni is currently spreading Karate in Osaka; this Soke is strongly linked to Shito-Kai. This time, master Manzo Iwata, former President of Shito-Kai, spoke about Kenwa Mabuni and Shito-ryu; also mentioned that it exists in Osaka Kenei Mabuni, spreading Karate and considered as Soke.

Inside Shito-Kai, there are several groups, but Shito-Kai and Shito-ryu are being spread together.

Great Master Manzo Iwata
Kenwa Mabuni
Fujita Seiko

This report was written by Genzo Iwata, son of Master Iwata Manzo. Master Kenwa Mabuni was born in 1889 and died in 1952. Kenwa Mabuni founded Shito-ryu, currently one of the 4 strongest styles of the Federation.

Kenwa Mabuni moved from Okinawa to Tokyo and lived there for one year; the next year went to Osaka and started spreading Karate Shito-ryu, making Osaka the strongest quarter. But in Tokyo, mainly at the University of Toyo, remained Master Iwata which carried out a great expansion. After, many students which graduated from this University also expanded Karate, and the seed of Karate grew in Tokyo and its surroundings.

When Master Kenwa Mabuni died, his son Kenei received the Soke of Shito-ryu's nomination, but as leader of Karate Shito-ryu in the Western part remained Manzo Iwata. Master Iwata worked very hard in the formation of the All Japan Karatedo Federation in 1964. The chairmen of the four largest styles in the Federation were older people, but Master Iwata was very young when he took charge.

Osaka is for his son Kenei Mabuni and Tokyo is for Manzo Iwata,; said by Kenwa Mabuni (Iwata Genzo).

In 1941, Manzo Iwata was a student of Kenwa Mabuni when entered the University of Toyo; afterwards when finished college formed the Shito-Kai quarter at his house, to promote and spread Kenwa Mabuni's Karate or Shito-ryu style.

Mrs. Iwata says about Mr. Kenwa Mabuni: He is very tranquil and quiet when coming to my house; never speaks about Karate and never makes any ostentation about his knowledge, a very gentle person. Master Iwata, also because his information, never allowed anybody to see his personal training. Master Iwata used to say "it is not to demonstrate to anybody, it is for my own formation." Kenwa Mabuni always said, "Karate matters are told and demonstrated in the Dojo."

Manzo Iwata and Seiko Fujita and Kenwa Mabuni: so respectful, was very active in the study of martial arts; formed a group for the study of Karate. He studied any martial art that surged at the time, always looking for the positive. In Karate there were no protectors but he studied the way to create them on behalf of students.

Master Kenwa Mabuni made relations with all persons and styles, with open mind and positiveness. This is how Manzo Iwata and Fujita engaged with Master Kenwa Mabuni.

First, my father studied Bo with Master Kenwa Mabuni, says Genzo, but the Master said to Manzo Iwata to study Jo instead of Bo. There, he introduced him to Seiko Fujita, begining a relation between Master Iwata and Master Fujita. Afterwards together with these two Masters, he started training Daien-ryu Jodo, Nanban Satoryu Kempo and Shingetsu Ryu Shuriken in parallel and received the heritage of Soke from the Masters.

Seiko Fujita, Kogaryu Ninjutsu 14th Soke, demonstrated his technical superiority and was known and called "the mysterious man of the martial art." He only accepted Master Manzo Iwata as student. At that time, there were also demonstrations that were not real, but Master Fujita always performed his demonstration with reason and truth. He wrote many books, but his knowledge was transmitted only to Master Manzo Iwata.

Master Manzo Iwata leaves his knowledge to his son Genzo Iwata. He has a dojo at home and there are always foreigner Masters training. When Genzo was a kid, he used to train with these students at the age of 10; his father never forced him since he used to say "only learns the one who is willing to learn." Master Manzo Iwata always expected the student's initiative, to ask, to learn, he always taught willingly.

The specialty of Shito-ryu is kata's Bunkai Kumite; Shito-ryu style looks for the technique with rationale, minimum movement with maximum effect;, contraction is very important as well as force and to avoid wasting energy in vain. This technique is achieved with correct positions. This is what my father used to say.

Satoryu Kempo, its technique has no name, only within Bunkai Kumite practice, this part is Satoryu. This is the way I was taught. Bunkai Kumite was taught by Kenwa Mabuni but some parts were changed for Sato Ryu style. Master Mabuni, then, took this style in some parts that fitted with reason, specially gyaku waza and nage waza.

Master Iwata did not make his living out of his martial arts, but dedicated more time to Karate than to tea manufacturing. I, Genzo Iwata, grew that way and learned that Karate is a very important part in our lives, but some times I compare the way I was taught by my father and my way, and see his teachings were so great.

I received from my father Sho Shin Sho Gai, it means to learn Karate show your mind clear and courteous all your life, with eagerness to learn more since there is no limit; this is the word of Sho Shin Sho Gai.

Picture No. 4
1944-Master Iwata Manzo received from Kenwa Mabuni his diploma of Shito-ryu Karate-do.
Picture No. 5
1948-Master Manzo Iwata receives his diploma from Seiko Fujita Shihan.
Picture No. 6
1943-Master Iwata Daien Ryu Jodo's diploma received from Seiko Fujita.

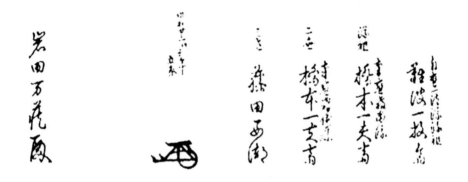

Left portion of Nanban Satto-ryu Kempo densho designated
as picture No. 5 in Iwata Genzo's letter

Copy of Daien-ryu densho designated as picture No. 6
in Iwata Genzo's letter.

One page translation of 1995 "Nihon Kobudo Taikai" program, page 151:

38—Nanban Satto-ryu Kempo [ ]

Headmaster [Soke]:   Iwata Genzo
Address: Iruma City, Saitama Prefecture
Telephone:

Transmission Lineage from the Founder:

(Ancestral Origins [Genso])
Hashimoto Ippusai (1ˢᵗ generation) → Hashimoto Ippusai (2ⁿᵈ generation) → Fujita
Seiko → Iwata Manzo → Iwata Genzo

Tradition Outline:

A warrior from Satsuma, Hashimoto Ippusai is the founder [Kaiso]. He used this art actively during the battle of *Toba Fushimi* [1868; Kyoto]. The second generation inheritor [nidai] also took the name Hashimoto Ippusai, and was in turn succeeded by the third generation inheritor [sandai] Fujita Seiko, who was referred to as "the last ninja," being the 14ᵗʰ generation of Koga-ryu ninjutsu.

The 4ᵗʰ generation inheritor [yondai] was Iwata Manzo, who received full transmission [menkyo kaiden] in Shito-ryu Karate-do, as well as succession of the arts Daien-ryu jojutsu and Shingetsu-ryu shurikenjutsu.

The art teaches how to successfully combine strikes [atemi], throwing techniques [nage waza], and locking techniques [Kansetsu waza] while encouraging the flexibility to adapt them freely to an infinite amount of applications. All the techniques consist of straight line movements and were created for actual fighting. As such, many techniques are dangerous and are passed down from headmaster to headmaster only [isshi soden].

July 28th, 2004

Dear Phillip,

Please find enclosed translations of the Nanban satto-ryu sections of the 1990 and 1995 Nihon Kobudo Taikai program books, as well as .pdf's of the originals. I went ahead and formatted the translation a bit, and scanned the one photo that was included in the first program.

Words in brackets "[ ]" are either the Japanese term used for the preceding text for your reference or relevant comments that may be of interest from myself not found in the original text. We were able to confirm all the romanization of the kanji through a variety of methods, one of which was to call the phone number provided in Japan and ask them directly. This is significant because the Iwata's were direct students of Fujita Sensei, and would have first hand knowledge with how such names and terms are pronounced. What we translated turned out to be correct, which is reassuring, but there are a couple of things that are worth mentioning since I noticed that there seems to be some confusion various places on the net. "Nanban Satto-ryu kempo" is the correct romanization of the art name. "Nanban" means "barbarian south", and used to refer to a number of countries near Japan (ie: China). "Satto" means to "swarm upon", or "come down on", and is a term commonly used in Japanese language. Also, though "Saiko" is a more logical reading of Fujita's first name, it was in fact pronounced "Seiko" (many references I found are spelling it "Saiko").

The Iwata's are not really teaching the art any more, so I don't know if it is still a living art or not.

I hope you find this translation interesting and useful. If you have any further translation projects—letters, books, magazine articles, scrolls, web pages, etc.—please feel free to contact us. This mailing concludes our translation project agreement.

Regards,
Nathan Scott
Tae Iio

DISAPPEAR . . . 'THE LAST NINJA'"

"A half-life of Seiko Fujita, Kouga-ryu Ninjutsu 14th Generation"

> "The last Ninja who lived in a modern society." On 4th, Seiko Fujita (66), Kouga-ryu Ninjutsu 14th generation, passed away caused by cirrhosis of the liver at his house, Nezu 1-24-3, Bunkyo-ku, Tokyo. Because he did not have an inheritor, the orthodox Ninja and Ninjutsu were practically ended in Japan. An article below shows a half-life of the last Ninja.

"Ending A Life of 66 Years"

Fujita's funeral was held from noon at Kanou-in Temple in Daitou-ku (Tokyo). Like Konishi (Sindou Munen-ryu Kenjutsu) who was the chairperson of the funeral committee, Japanese traditional martial artists lined up for the funeral with regretting a death of the last Ninja.

Due to the appearance of Ninja actors, who performed very much like actual Ninja, in TV and movies in the Ninja boom last year, people no longer believed Ninjutsu as a technique which simply "makes oneself disappear by just performing *IN* (interlacing fingers)." Nonetheless, it was doubtful that ordinary people knew real Ninjutsu like a technique in which one could go in and out a 20 centimeter chinks in the wall. Ninjutsu, which was perhaps effectively used in the disturbances of war, was unnecessary and unrealistic to modern people now although they valued Ninja stories in TV, movies, or novels for the purpose of getting rid of their stress by watching them.

It was perhaps difficult for us to believe the existence of Ninja due to luck of chance to observe Ninjutsu in our daily life.

"No Inheritor: Putting an End to Ninja by the Fujita's Generation"

According to Fujita's book, *Doron Doron*, unless one had great patience and right-minded, one could not master Ninjutsu. In order to be Ninja, one needed to have

a lot of practices and to be good at all martial arts (Fujita was the third generation
of Nanban Sattou-ryu, a master of Singetsu-ryu Shuriken jutsu, a master of Daien-
ryu Jou jutsu, and a master of Ichiden-ryu Hoshu jutsu). In addition, one could not
be taught Ninjutsu unless he/she had right-minded due to the usage of dangerous
poisons that could make a blood clot on one's heart by one drop on his/her skin for
an assassination.

"Difficulties to Get a Ninja Qualification"

If a wicked person were able to use Ninjutsu, there would be a lot of thieves like
Goemon Ishikawa who was one of the cleverest thieves in Japan. Because of this
kind of reason, a Ninja never taught Ninjutsu to even his/her own child if he/she
believed that his/her child was not talented enough to be a Ninja mentally and
physically.

Therefore, unlike Kenjutsu or Jujutsu which were developed during wartime under
the pressure of necessity, Ninjutsu gradually disappeared as time passed. Recently, Ninja
Fujita, who was the last Ninja in Japan, passed away. As a result, Ninja disappeared
forever from this world.

"An Inimitable Swashbuckler: Fighting with A Saber on His Hand at the Age of Six"

Fujita's ancestor worked for . . . Shogun as a secret agent and their leader led by
the shogunate and lived around Kouga-cho, Kanda, Chiyota-ku in Tokyo at the current
address. Shin-nosuke Fujita, who was Seiko's father (died in July 15, Shouwa ?, at the
age of 64), was expert in catching criminals by using and tying with ropes. He worked
as "a detective at the Metropolitan Police Department Investigation. Until he retired
in Meiji 45, he caught a famous criminal and Peeping Toms. In addition, he worked
well for catching eight condemned criminals and 25 criminals who were sentenced
in imprisonment for life. He was a person whom people expressed him in a song,
"Detective Fujita is scarier than ogres, demons, and monsters."

Shintasaemon, Fujita's grandfather, was the 13th generation of Kouga-Ryu Ninja.
Fujita had learned Ninjutsu such as Hokou-jutsu (walking techniques) and Chouyaku-
Jutsu (jumping techniques) from his grandfather since he was three or four.

There was an episode (described by Fujita's friend K) about Fujita's childhood;

"Fujita was six years old when his father worked at a police substation in Oume,
[Tokyo]. One day, Fujita saw his brother was beat up by naughty boys and came back
home with his ears bleeding. Fujita pulled out a saber which was hanged on the wall
in a room and went for the revenge. He swung a saber around toward those naughty
boys who were screaming and running away and neighbors who rushed to come to
the place after hearing these kids screaming. The neighbors knocked his saber down
and caught him. He hurt 11 people totally."

This incident was not made public because it was done by the six years old boy. However, Fujita's father shaved Seiko's head to show his apologies to public and sent him to a temple in Itsuka-shi.

"Hard Training in Ninjutsu; Learned from His Grandfather"

If Fujita were an ordinary child, he would be quiet after the incident. However, he was back to be mischievous a few months later. While the chief priest of the Buddhist temple was away, Fujita invited his naughty friends into the main building of the temple. They rang the temple bell and a wood block as much as they wanted. They took the statue of the Buddha down and put horse manures instead. Sometimes, they put wax on a hallway and made monks slip over on the hallway. In other time, Fujita surprised those monks by making fireworks. After giving monks a great deal of trouble, he was sent back to home approximately after one year.

In summary by people who were close to him, he began to learn Ninjutsu officially/truly from his grandfather right after came back home from the temple. Although his grandfather was soft on Fujita usually, he was very strict about teaching Ninjutsu. Fujita got often injured by the practice. However, he continued practicing Ninjutsu by bracing himself up for a fight. Before the age of thirteen when he lost his grandfather in fall, his grandfather taught him the bases of Kouga-ryu.

Off course meanwhile, Fujita continued to be mischievous. He surprised other people by fighting with *Yakuza* and jumping from a second floor at school.

Before his grandfather died, he called Fujita at his bedside and gave two volumes of Ninja scrolls. When he gave it to Fujita, he left words; "the orthodox Kouga-ryu will be ended after you." After the death of his grandfather, Fujita tried to complete Ninjutsu training for not to disappoint his grandfather.

Two months later, Fujita left home. He lived with Yamabushi. He spent a lot of time to practice and to improve his self-defense techniques at noon and night. He mastered Ninjutsu gradually.

"If he drunk sake, he could drink eight bottles and half (14.6 liters); he ate 25 bowls of plain buckwheat noodles in soup"

By the way, Fujita, a daredevil, was to be reckoned with in good form as usual. After graduating from Soujitsu in 1914, he enrolled in Waseda University, Tokyo University and Meiji University. However, he was kicked out from these universities due to his violent behavior. He finally earned a degree in religions from Nippon University in 1919. Not only he was enrolled at these universities, but also did he work as a journalist in newspaper publishing companies such as the *Houchi*, the *Hibi*(?), the *Yamato*, the *Kokumin*, and the *Chugai*. In addition to that, he was teaching Judo and Kendo.

Fujita was not just a daredevil. It seemed that he was smart. He held professional positions in teaching at Toyama School, Rikudai (the abbreviation for a university of the

Military), and Kaidai (the abbreviation for a university of Marine) after he graduating from Nippon University. Until recently, he was a trustee of Nihon Kobudo Koushin Kai. At an exhibition game in Kobudou which was held once in a year, he presented a wealth of his knowledge and his experiences for the audience to understand what Kobudou was in general.

Before Fujita died, he expressed, "one has to spend practicing Ninjustu in one's whole life. There is no completion in one's practice. In fact, I have practiced martial arts for fifty years, but I still need to practice more. Based on his statement, it was clear that he was strict to himself.

This was the reason why he was called "the last Ninja."

Many people introduced or were introduced themselves Ninja as if they were taking advantage of the trend of the recent Ninja boom. However, Fujita claimed that they were not real Ninja.

If they had a long cloth around their neck while they were running 60 kilometers in a day, which Ninja considered as a walk, it would be interesting to know how many of them could run without touching the tip of the cloth on the ground.

"Eating Bricks"

Ninja ate a special kind of food frequently to kill his/her body odor so that they could keep from being seen by his/her enemy. There was perhaps no possibility among those people, who claimed themselves as Ninja, could fast and gorge themselves with food and drink like Fujita who had records of drinking eight bottles and half (14.6 liters) and eating 25 bowls of plain buckwheat noodles in soup. In case of eating voraciously, Ninja could control involuntary muscles in a stomach by training. It was understandable that people considered Fujita "eccentric" by seeing his eccentric behavior.

Fujita's unusual episodes never ended. For example, he was worshiped as a "living god." In other time, he terrified *Yakuza*, who picked up a fight with him, by forcing them to eat the flesh of his thigh after he scooped it out by himself. In another time, he competed with a huge man for physical strength. At that time, the huge man weighted 157.5 kilograms and claimed himself as "the most powerful man in the world." It was unfortunate that Ninjutsu, which was a Japanese unique martial art, died away.

"People Who were Closed to Fujita Mourned His Death: A Funeral Service Amidst The Hush of Deep Sorrow on 11th"

Zenya (?) Kunii (a master of Kagoshima Shindou-Ryu Kenjutsu), who was a friend of Fujita, attended his funeral and said, "as a consequence of Fujita's death, Ninjutsu completely disappeared. Because he was also famous for researching ancient writings, we deplored his death more than we could say. However, we believe in the immortality of his soul. We believe that his spirit will guide us including his descendants in a good way somehow."

Nanban Sattou-ryu Kenpoo succeeded Manzou Iwata as the 4th generation after Fujita who was the 3rd generation. Iwata commented that "we were under the care of our teacher [Fujita] not just martial arts but also in all ways. Losing him suddenly before we repaid his generosity and courtesy was like we lost an important thing in our mind. However, we will overcome this sadness and continue developing the traditional martial arts (*Kobudoo*) with spending our efforts.

Ryushou (?) Sakagami, a master of Sishuu (?)-ryu Karate, looked regretted and said that "Fujita was the last person who was fully perservering in his training. All Ninjutsu including Kouga-ryu Ninpoo disappeared forever."

People who attended Fujita's funeral were Ryuji Kiyomizu/Shimizu (Sindou Musou-ryu joudou), Sei Kobayashi (Toda-ha Bukou-ryu Naginata ?), Toki Ikeda (Tendou-ryu Naginata ?), Masaru ? Watanabe (Kenyuu/Genyuu-ryu Karate), Akira/Toshi Saitou (Kongan-ryu Shuriken), Kiyonobu? Ogasawara (Ogasawa-ryu Kyuujutsu), Motokatsu? Inoue (Okinawa Kobudou Karate), Tani Chojiro (Tani-ha Shito-ryu Karate), Hon Reik? (Musou-ryu Joujutsu), Jjusei Ono (Ono-ha Ittou-ryu). In all cases, these people had highly qualified in martial arts.

Captions

Fujita, who was called as the last Ninja

Fujita during his lifetime. In order to show the spirit of Ninja, he pricked his body with so many needles, even yoga ascetics were dumbfounded.

The secret scroll of Ninja

Ninja standing up quietly and his dark shadow cast on the *fusuma* (a papered sliding door). Ninja had this style for the most part.

Manzou Iwata, who became the 4th generation in Nanban Sattou-ryu

The funeral was held in Kanou-in Temple at Yasunaka (?), Tokyo

BIBLIOGRAPHY

Anonymous: The Last Ninja Disappears (The Obituary of Fujita Seiko), Ninkan Kanko, 1/14/1966
Anonymous: Togakure-ryu in 007, Tokyo Times, 3/6/1966
Adams, Andrew: Last of The Ninja, Black Belt, 2/1967
Adams, Andrew: Ninja Technique, Black Belt, 3/1967
Adams, Andrew: Ninja: The Invisible Assassins, 1970
Cunningham, Don: Taiho-Jutsu: Law and Order in the Age of the Samurai, 2004
Draeger, Donn F: Classical Budo Vol II, New York, 1973
_____ Comprehensive Asian Fighting Arts, 1981
Durbin, William: Ninjutsu: A Different Perspective
Ettig, Wolfgang: Toshitsugu Takamatsu: The Last Shinobi, Schmitten, 2006
Fujita, Seiko: Ninjutsu Hiroku, Tokyo 1936
_____ Watashi Wa Ninjutsu, "Liberal," Tokyo 1952
_____ Kenpo Gokui Atemi No Sakkatsu-Ho Meikai, Tokyo, 1958
_____ Koga-ryu Ninja Ichidaiki, Tokyo, 1968
Guintard, Sylvain: Fujita Saiko: Stranger Than Truth, Karate-Bushido, Translated by Patrick Lombardo
_____ Master Fujita Seiko: The last True Ninja, *http://members.shaw.ca/shugendo/namban.html*
Hevener, Phillip: *http://fujitaseiko.tripod.com*
Inoue, Motokatsu: Interview, SOKN magazine No. 2, 2002
Iwata Genzo: Letter to Sam Moledzki
McCarthy, Patrick, Ancient Okinawan Martial Arts: Koryu Uchinadi, 1999
Mercado, Stephen: Shadow Warriors of Nakano, Dulles, 2002
Mitose, James M: What Is Self Defense (Kenpojuijutsu), 1953
_____ In Search of Kenpo 1984
Moikawa, Tetsuro, Budo Nippon, Tokyo Press, 1964
Mol, Serge: Classical Fighting Arts of Japan, New York, 2001
Moledzki, Sam: *http://www.shitoryu.org*
Murayama, Kunio: Private Interview, 9/10/2005
Nihon Kobudo Shinkokai: Enbu Taikai Program-Nanban Satto-ryu Kempo, 1990 & 1995

Noble, Graham: Motobu Choki: A Real Fighter, Fighting Arts Intl No. 32 Vol6, No.2, 1988

Oda, Hirohisa: Real Ninja, San Ramon, 2002

Plee, Henri: L'Art Sublime et Ultime des Points Vitaux, Nosiy-sur-Ecole, 1998

Roley, Don: History of Koga Ryu, *http://www.jigokudojo.com/koga.htm*

Tomizuka, Makoto: (Translator) The Last Ninja Disappears, Fujita Seiko

Turnbull, Stephen: Ninja: The True Story of Japan's Secret Warrior Cult, New York, 1992

Salone, Samuel: Ninjutsu: They Knew All About Poison Gas, Journal of Non-lethal Combatives, December 1999.

Scott, Nathan: (Translator) Nihon Kobudo Shinkokai: Enbu Taikai Program, 1990 & 1995

Sullivan, John: Inoue: Master of Kobujutsu, "Fighting Arts" Vol. 2, No. 6, 1976

Svinth, Joseph: Documentation Regarding The Budo Ban in Japan, 1945-1950, Journal of Combative Sport, December 2002.

Watatani, Kiyoshi/Yamada Tadashi: Bugei Ryuha Daijiten, 1978

NOTES

Chapter 1: **UNSETTELED YOUTH**

[1]   Fujita, Seiko, Koga Ryu Ichidaiki, p.13

[2]   Fujita, Seiko, Watashi Wa Ninjutsu Tsukai, "Liberal," 1952.

[3]   Obituary of Fujita Seiko: The Last Ninja Disappears, Nikan Kanko, 1/14/1966.

[4]   Fujita, Seiko, Koga Ryu Ninja Ichidaiki, p. 14.

[5]   Obituary of Fujita Seiko: The Last Ninja Disappears, Nikan Kanko, 1/14/1966.

[6]   Fujita, Seiko, Koga Ryu Ninja Ichidaiki, p 14.

[7]   ibid, p.15.

[8]   ibid, p.14.

[9]   ibid, p.15.

[10] ibid, p.16.

[11] ibid, p.17.

[12] ibid, p.17.

Chapter 2: **LIVING WITH THE YAMABUSHI**

[13] Fujita, Seiko, Koga Ryu Ninja Ichidaiki, p.18

[14] Watatani, Kiyoshi/Yamada Kiyoshi, Bugei Ryuha Daijiten, P. 509.

[15] Fujita, Seiko, Koga Ryu Ninja Ichidaiki, pp. 24-32.

Chapter 3: **THE LAST DISCIPLE OF THE WADA-HA**

[16] Fujita, Seiko, Koga Ryu Ninja Ichidaiki, p.34

[17] Watatani, Kiyoshi/Yamada Tadashi, Bugei Ryuha Daijiten, p. 921.

[18] Turnbull, Stephen, Ninja: The True Story of Japan's Secret Warrior Cult, p. 32.

[19] Fujita, Seiko, Watashi Wa Ninjutsu Tsukai, "Liberal," 1952.

[20] Cunningham, Don, Taiho-Jutsu: Law and Order in the Age of the Samurai, p. 45-46.

[21] Fujita, Seiko, Watashi Wa Ninjutsu Tsukai, "Liberal," 1952.

Chapter 4: **TRAINING WITH THE MASTER**

[22]   Guintard, Sylvain, Master Fujita Seiko: The Last True Ninja.

[23]   Fujita, Seiko, Koga Ryu Ninja Ichidaiki, p. 34-35.

[24]   ibid, p.37.

[25]   ibid, p.38

[26]   ibid, p.38.

[27]   ibid, p.39.

[28]   ibid, p. 39.

[29]   ibid, p. 40.

[30]   ibid, p.40.

[31]   ibid, pp. 40-41.

[32]   ibid, p. 41.

[33]   ibid, p.41.

[34]   ibid, p.43.

[35]   ibid, p. 45.

[36]   ibid, p. 46.

[37]   ibid, pp. 47-49.

Chapter 5: **FINAL LESSONS**

[38]   Fujita, Seiko, Koga Ryu Ninja Ichidaiki, p.56.

[39]   ibid, p. 57.

[40]   ibid, p. 57.

[41]   ibid, p. 58.

[42]   ibid, p. 59.

[43]   ibid, p. 56.

[44]   The Last Ninja Disappears, Ninkan Kanko, 1/14/1966, Fujita, Seiko, Koga Ryu Ninja Ichidaiki, p.57.

[45]   ibid.

[46]   ibid.

Chapter 6: **THE YOUNG SEEKER**

[47]   Guintard, Sylvain, Master Fujita Saiko: The Last True Ninja.

[48]   Fujita, Seiko, Watashi Wa Ninjutsu Tsukai, "Liberal," 1952.

[49]   Fujita Seiko, Koga Ryu Ninja Ichidaiki, P. 51.

[50]   ibid, p. 52.

[51]   ibid, p. 54.

[52]   ibid, p. 55.

[53]   ibid, p. 56.

[54]   Fujita, Seiko, Watashi Wa Ninjutsu Tsukai, "Liberal," 1952.

Chapter 7: **THE FORMATIVE YEARS**

[55] The Last Ninja Disappears, Nikan Kanko, 1/14/1966.

[56] ibid.

[57] ibid.

[58] Guintard, Sylvain, Fujita Saiko: Stranger Than Truth, Karate-Bushido.

[59] Guintard, Sylvain, Master Saiko Fujita: The Last True Ninja.

Chapter 8: **NANBAN SATTO RYU KEMPO**

[60] Mol, Serge, Classical Fighting Arts of Japan: A Complete Guide to Koryu Jujutsu, p. 51.

[61] Guintard, Sylvain, Fujita Saiko: The Last True Ninja.

[62] Fujita, Seiko, Watashi Wa Ninjutsu Tsukai, "Liberal," 1952.

[63] Watatani, Kiyoshi/Yamada, Tadashi, Bugei Ryuha Daijiten, p.662.

[64] Nanban Satto-ryu Kempo: Nihon Kobudo Shinkokai Enbu Taikai Program, p. 151, 1995.

[65] ibid, p. 151.

[66] Durbin, William, Ninjutsu: A Different Perspective.

[67] ibid.

[68] Noble, Graham, Motobu Choki: A Real Fighter, Fighting Arts International, No. 32, Vol. 6, No. 2, pp. 10-17, 1986.

[69] ibid pp. 10-17.

[70] Ettig, Wolfgang, Toshitsugu Takamatsu: The Last Shinobi, p. 268.

[71] Guintard, Sylvain, Private e-mail correspondence related to his claim to having learned Nanban Satto-ryu Kempo while living in Japan between 1989-2001. Sylvain states that he was taught by Fujita's son-in-law, Fujita Yoshi, who is not documented in any of the official martial art sources.

[72] Nanban Satto-ryu Kempo: Ninhon Kobudo Shinkokai Enbu Taikai Program, p. 151, 1995.

[73] Murayama, Kunio, Private interview related to his discipleship and Iwata Manzo, 9/10/2005.

[74] Iwata, Genzo, Letter to Sam Moledzki, responding to Moledzki's inquiries into the career of his father, Iwata Manzo.

Chapter 9: **THE WAR YEARS**

[75] Ettig, Wolfgang, Toshitsugu Takamatsu: The Last Shinobi, p.231

[76] Guintard, Sylvain, Master Saiko Fujita: The Last True Ninja.

[77] Mercado, Stephen, Shadow Warriors of Nakano, p. 94.

[78] ibid, p. 95.

[79] ibid, p. 95.

[80] Oda, Horihisa, Real Ninja, p. 94.

[81] Plee Henri, L'Art Sublime et Ultime des Points, p.60

[82] ibid, p. 62.

[83] ibid, p. 62.

84 ibid, p. 6.
85 Mercado, Stephen, Shadow Warriors of Nakano, p.162.
86 Roley, Don, History of Koga Ryu.
87 Iwata, Genzo, Letter to Sam Moledzki, photocopy of Daien-ryu menkyo kaiden was included in letter.

Chapter 10: FUJITA: RESPECTED MARTIAL ARTIST

88 The Last Ninja Disappears, Nikan Kanko, 1/14/1966.
89 Morikawa, Tetsuru, Budo Nippon, p. 106.
90 Moledzki, Sam, Interview related to his apprenticeship to Sakagami Ryusho. Moledzki learned Iaido, kubudo, and karate from Sakagami.
91 Ettig, Wolfgang, Toshistsugu Takamatsu: The Last Shinobi, p. 157.
92 ibid, p.268.
93 Draeger, Donn F. Comprehensive Asian Fighting Arts, p. 193.
94 ibid, p. 130.
95 McCarthy, Patrick, Ancient Okinawan Martial Arts: Koryu Uchinadi, p. 43.
96 Fujita, Seiko, Watashi Wa Ninjutsu Tsuaki, "Liberal," 1952.
97 Inoue Motokatsu Interview, SOKN Magazine No. 2, 2002.
98 Ryukyukobudo.com: Lineage Chart.

Chapter 11: SAVING BUJUTSU

99   The Last Ninja Disappears, Nikan Kanko, 1/14/1966.
100 Svinth, Joseph, Documentation Regarding The Budo Ban In Japan, 1945-1950, Journal of Combative Sport, December 2002.
101 ibid.
102 Guintard, Sylvain, Master Saiko Fujita: The Last True Ninja.
103 Svith, Joseph, Documentation Regarding The Budo Ban In Japan, 1945-1950, Journal of Combative Sport, December 2002.
104 Moledzki, Sam, Shitoryu.org.
105 Guintard, Sylvain, Master Saiko Fujita: The Last True Ninja.
106 Sullivan, John, Inoue: Master of Kobujutsu, "Fighting Arts" Vol.2, No. 6. pp. 23-27, 1976.

Chapter 12: PASSING ON THE SYSTEMS

107 The Last Ninja Disappears, Nikan Kanko, 1/14/1966.
108 Watatani, Kiyoshi/Yamada, Tadashi, Bugei Ryuha Daijiten, p. 662, Nanban Satto-ryu Kempo p.509, Daien-ryu Jojutsu, p. 401, Shingetsu-ryu: Fujita's name does not appear in this listing, although his claim was widely accepted.
109 Inoue Motokatsu Interview: SOKN magazine No. 2, 2002.
110 Sullivan, John, Inoue: Master of Kobujutsu, "Fighting Arts" Vol.2, No. 6. pp. 23-27, 1976

[111] ibid.

[112] ibid.

[113] ibid.

[114] ibid.

[115] ibid.

[116] The Last Ninja Disappears, Nikan Kanko, 1/14/1966.

[117] ibid.

[118] Iwata, Genzo, Letter to Sam Moledzki, responding to Moledzki's inquiries into the career of Iwata Manzo.

[119] Watatani, Kiyoshi/Yamada Tadashi, Bugei Ryuha Daijiten, pp. 662, 509. Ninhon Kobudo Shinkokai Enbu Taikai Program, p. 151, 1995.

[120] Moledzki, Sam, Shitoryu.org.

Chapter 13: **THE LAST KOGA NINJA**

[121] Watatani, Kiyoshi/Yamada, Tadashi, Bugei Ryuha Daijiten, p. 273.

[122] ibid, p. 273.

[123] Adams, Andrew, Ninja: The Invisible Assassins, p. 173.

[124] Watanti, Kiyoshi/Yamada, Tadashi, Bugei Ryuha Daijiten, p. 921.

[125] ibid, p. 273.

Chapter 14: **PRESERVING THE ART'S INTEGRITY**

[126] Draeger, Donn F. Classical Budo: The Martial Arts and Ways of Japan, Vol. 2, p. 19.

[127] Fujita Seiko, Watashi Wa Ninjutsu Tsukai, "Liberal," 1952.

[128] Togakure-ryu to be in 007, Tokyo Times, 3/6/1966, Translation by Benjamin Cole.

[129] Adams, Andrew, Last of The Ninja, 2/1967, Ninja Technique, 3/1967, Black Belt.

[130] Salone, Samuel, Ninjutsu: They Knew All About Poison Gas, Journal of Non-lethal Combatives, December 1999.

[131] Turnbull, Stephen, Ninja: The True Story of Japan's Secret Warrior Cult, p. 144.

[132] The Last Ninja Disappears, Nikan Kanko, 1/14/1966.

[133] Adams, Andrews, Ninja: The Invisible Assassins, p. 173.

[134] Turnbull, Stephen, Ninja: The True Story of Japan's Secret Warrior Cult, p. 148.

[135] Moledzki, Sam, Private Communication: Moledzki donated photos of various Iwata family items bequeathed to Iwata Manzo by Fujita Seiko.

[136] Fujita, Seiko, Ninjutsu Hiroku, Inside cover illustration of ukiyo-e, which is included in photos taken by Jose Luis Caledroni while studying with Iwata Manzo, and which were later donated to this project by Sam Moledzki.

[137] Moledzki, Sam, Shitoryu.org.

[138] Iwata, Genzo, Letter to Sam Moledzki, responding to Moledzki's inquiries into the career of his father, Iwata Manzo.

[139] The Last Ninja Disappears, Nikan Kanko, 1/14/1966.

Chapter 15: **FUJITA'S LEGACY**

[140]   Hevener, Phillip, Fujita Seiko: The Last Koga Ninja, *http://fujitaseiko.tripod.com.*

[141]   The Last Ninja Disappears, Nikan Kanko, 1/14/1966.

[142]   Ninhon Kobudo Shinkokai Enbu Taikai Program, p. 151, 1995.

[143]   Adams, Andrew, Last of The Ninja, Black Belt, p. 33, 2/1967.

PHOTO CREDITS

1. Fujita Bunko, Michael Sloan, at author's request.
2. Ninujtsu Hisho Ogiden no Kan, Michael Sloan, at author's request.
3. Iwata, Fujita, Mabuni, military picture. Sam Moledzki.
4. Nanban Satto-ryu scroll, Sam Moledzki.
5. Fujita, Taira, Sakagami, Inoue, Sam Moldzki.
6. Koga/Iga Ninjutsu Hikan Banseshukai, Sam Moldezki.
7. Obituary of Fujita Seiko, Nikan Kanko, Sam Moledzki.
8. Iwata family armour picture, Sam Moledzki.
9. Daien-ryu Menkyo Kaiden, Appendix, Sam Moledzki.
10. Cover Image, Ukiyo-e from Ninjutsu Hiroku, Sam Moldezki.
11. Nanban Satto-ryu Kempo (Left side of densho) photocopy, Appendix, Sam Moledzki.

Lightning Source UK Ltd.
Milton Keynes UK
17 August 2010

158545UK00002B/80/P